Introduction

Each offseason, the National Football League (NFL) holds an event now known as the NFL Combine, which showcases the best 300 NFL prospects in the country. The NFL Combine includes medical tests, interviews, and a multitude of athletic tests, drills, and evaluations. The Combine participants include mostly college juniors and seniors who are selected based on how their college careers translate to the NFL. And while on-field game evaluations are probably the most important component of a prospect's NFL Draft evaluation, the NFL Combine offers a venue for standardized tests of athleticism under controlled conditions which allow for unbiased and consistent comparisons of athleticism between prospects. These standardized drills are implemented to measure how fast, agile, explosive, and strong prospects are. A brief description of each primary athletic test is listed below.

40-yard dash

The 40-yard dash is unequivocally the most popular event at the combine. The 40-yard dash is meant to measure an athlete's linear speed, acceleration, explosion from a static start, and even running form or gait. Athletes are timed at 10, 20 and 40-yard intervals.

Bench press

The bench press test is for max-repetitions with 225 pounds on a flat bench press. This drill measures both upper body strength and strength endurance, and can indicate how much time an athlete spent on strength and conditioning in college.

Vertical leap

The vertical leap is an ideal showcase for lower-body explosion, power, and force production. During this drill, an athlete will stand flat-footed, measure their reach, and perform a full counter-movement jump.

Broad jump

Like the vertical leap, the broad jump will also test an athlete's lower-body explosion and power. The broad jump also measures force in the horizontal direction, balance, and coordination through the jump and landing. The athlete will begin from a standing position, and then explode out as far as they can in the horizontal direction.

3 cone drill

The 3 cone drill tests an athlete's ability to change directions while running at a high speed, and making 90° turns. Three cones are oriented in an L-shape. The prospect will start from the starting line, sprint 5 yards to the first cone and return to the starting line, turn around and run back to the first cone, take a 90° turn, sprint 5 yards to the second cone which he weaves around, and sprints back to the starting line while turning around the middle cone. Hopefully the schematic below helps to explain this drill better than I did.

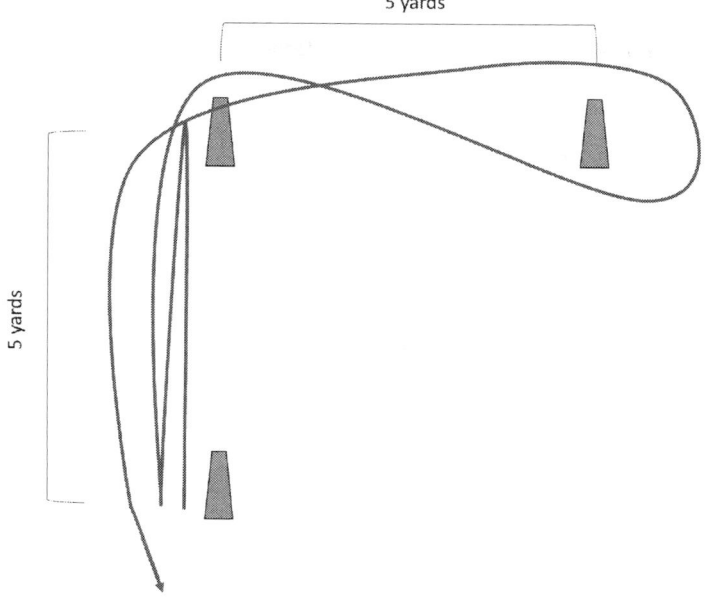

Shuttle run

The shuttle run (or short shuttle) is a classic shuttle run in which the athletes begins the drill, sprints 5 yards in one direction, reverses direction, sprints 10 yards in the opposite direction, reverses direction again, and finishes the drill by running 5 more yards to the finish line. The shuttle run tests the athlete's lateral quickness, acceleration, change of direction ability, ability to stop, balance, agility, and explosion in short areas.

***

So how important are these tests? And what do they tell us about an NFL prospect's potential?

Well, that is basically the entire premise of this book. From an analytical and quantitative perspective, this book will walk you through some of the greatest athletic feats ever at the NFL Combine. I will discuss what athletic traits appear to be statistically important in talent evaluations, and which ones don't. And lastly, I will provide some examples for how scouts or NFL personnel departments can borrow from other scientific disciplines to help them interpret NFL Combine data. The purpose of this book is not to evangelize the "analytics" movement, or to exaggerate the usefulness of the NFL Combine. At its core, the NFL Combine is a spectacle. It is a controlled showcase of athletic ability measured by drills that are quite different than an actual game of football. But, the data does tell us something. And there is still so much more potential in interpreting that data. The joy in writing this book has simply been rooted in the questions I ask. I'm just a curious person who loves football, numbers, and I'm fascinated by physical freaks of nature. And, hopefully the end of this book, you will be a little more curious about what you are watching each February in Indy.

Legends of the NFL Combine

During the offseason of 1982, National Football Scouting, Inc. held the first National Invitational Camp in balmy Tampa, Florida to help organize and facilitate multiple teams in evaluating NFL prospects. Tex Schramm, the former president and GM of the Dallas Cowboys, proposed choosing a central location for scouting camps to simplify the talent evaluation process for NFL teams. So, starting in 1982, The National Invitational Camp would hold small scouting camps in Tampa, New Orleans, and Arizona that representatives from multiple NFL teams could attend. Eventually, the National Invitational Camp moved permanently to Indianapolis in 1987, and became known as simply The NFL Scouting Combine. The NFL Combine is now a week-long exhibition that is held every February at Lucas Oil Stadium in Indianapolis, Indiana, and has developed into a full-blown media- and sponsor-backed spectacle for NFL hopefuls to showcase their athleticism.

With relatively little media attention in the early years, the Combine used to carry an underground or myth-like presence with it. Legends of Bo Jackson and Deion Sanders running sub-4.3s in the 40-yard dash were captivating for a football fan, but without verification, these stories were akin to pitch speeds from baseball's dead-ball era. Over the years, record keeping for Combine drills has improved. In fact, today the NFL Combine incorporates some of the most innovative technology in sports. One huge step forward in technology was when the NFL Combine began electronically timing the 40 yard dash in 1999, which allows accurate historical comparisons of players from any year after.

Once difficult to obtain, results from the NFL Combine are now streamed in entirety on The NFL Network, and updated continually through the week on ESPN. In fact, the NFL Combine draws more viewers than most NBA Playoff games. Today's attendees no longer wear sweats or athletic department-issued shorts from college, but are rather outfitted in all the latest sports performance wear that Under Armour has to offer. Adidas actually offers prospects the chance to win a Porsche if they run the fastest 40-yard dash…and are willing to sign an endorsement deal with the shoe company prior to running. The NFL Combine holds allure for nearly every football follower. Fans may watch the Combine in hopes that one of these special athletes are drafted by their team. Others may be intrigued by the other-worldly athleticism that these players possess in shorts and a t-shirt. Regardless of the reason, The NFL Combine is a showcase of extraordinary talent that seems to intrigue fans more and more each year.

Athletes attend the NFL Scouting Combine by invitation only. Redshirt sophomores, juniors, and seniors are eligible to be chosen by a selection committee. Up to 335 participants can be chosen by directors of both National Football Scouting and BLESTO scouting services. These two services combine to represent twenty-five NFL teams, and are joined by members of different NFL personnel departments in hopes of inviting every player drafted at that year's NFL Draft. From 2005 to 2014, invitations to the Combine were distributed by position as shown below.

NFL Scouting Combine Attendees by Percent (2005-2014)

Quarterbacks	6%
Running backs	10%
Wide receivers	14%
Tight ends	6%
Offensive linemen	16%
Defensive linemen	17%
Linebackers	10%
Defensive backs	18%
Kickers	3%

To fans, the most intriguing part of the NFL Combine is the on-field drills which measure the speed, strength, leaping ability, change of direction, and acceleration of each prospect. On-field drills include the 40-yard dash, broad jump, vertical jump, shuttle run, three-cone drill and bench press. In the last 15 years, there have been many outstanding performances in these on-field drills. However, like any population of people, there are always outliers. And some of the freakiest performances ever at the Combine are listed and discussed for each position below.

Notable Combine Performances 2003-2014

Position	Player	Height	Weight (lbs)	40 Yard Dash (secs)	Bench Reps (225 lb)	Vertical Leap (in)	Broad Jump (ft, in)
Quarterback	Robert Griffin III	6 ft 2⅜ in	223	4.38		39	10 ft 0 in
Running back	Brandon Jacobs	6 ft 4¼ in	267	4.56	19	37	9 ft 10 in
Wide receiver	Calvin Johnson	6 ft 5 in	239	4.35		42.5	11 ft 7 in
Tight End	Vernon Davis	6 ft 3¼ in	254	4.38	33	42	10 ft 8 in
Offensive Tackle	Lane Johnson	6 ft 6 in	303	4.72	28	34	9 ft 10 in
Offensive Guard	Bruce Campbell	6 ft 7 in	314	4.75	34	32	8 ft 5 in
Center	Ryan Kalil	6 ft 2 in	299	4.96	34	26	8 ft 8 in
Defensive Tackle	Aaron Donald	6 ft 1 in	275	4.68	35	32	9 ft 8 in
	Dontari Poe	6 ft 4 in	345	4.98	44	29.5	8 ft 9 in
Defensive End	Mario Williams	6 ft 7 in	295	4.66	35	40.5	10 ft 0 in
	J.J. Watt	6 ft 5 in	290	4.81	34	37	10 ft 0 in
Inside Linebacker	Luke Kuechly	6 ft 3 in	242	4.58	27	38.1	10 ft 3 in
Outside Linebacker	Demarcus Ware	6 ft 4 in	262	4.56	27	38.5	10 ft 7 in
Cornerback	Antonio Cromartie	6 ft 2 in	208	4.38	18	42	11 ft 0 in
Safety	Taylor Mays	6 ft 3 in	230	4.43	24	41	10 ft 5 in
Athlete	Matt Jones	6 ft 6$^{1/8}$ in	242	4.37		39.5	10 ft 9 in

Quarterback

Before joining Art Briles to re-write the Baylor football record book, Robert Griffin III broke Texas state records for the 110 and 300- meter hurdles in high school. His times of 13.55 seconds and 35.33 seconds were faster than those of fellow Texas track star Jamaal Charles in high school. Griffin III was 0.01 seconds away from tying a national high school record in the 300-meter hurdles. As a junior at Copperas Cove High School, Griffin III was named to the USA Today's All-USA Track and Field team, and was named the Gatorade Texas Track and Field Athlete of the Year. So naturally, Robert Griffin III went on to set school records for career passing yards, TDs, QB rating, and completion percentage at Baylor, all before being selected 2nd overall in the 2012 NFL Draft.

Running back

Brandon Jacobs is as large as NFL running backs get. In high school, Jacobs initially played defensive line and considered himself a better basketball player than football. At 6'4" tall and weighing 265 pounds, it is easy to see why he would begin his career in the trenches. However, Brandon Jacobs has extremely rare speed for his size, having been clocked running the 100 meter and 200 meter dashes in 10.82 and 21.59 seconds respectively. His 40 yard dash time of 4.56 and vertical leap of 37 inches make Brandon Jacobs truly one of the most uniquely physical backs ever.

Wide Receiver

Megatron. To garner a nickname like Megatron, an athlete must truly be inhuman. Anxiety and intrigue surrounded Calvin Johnson's weigh-in at the 2007 NFL Combine. After draft busts like USC's Mike Williams, general managers were growing weary of overgrown and out-of-shape wide receivers. At 6'5" tall, Johnson weighed in at nearly 240 pounds, resembling more a defensive end than a wide receiver. Adding to the concern over his weight, Johnson informed scouts that he would not run or workout at the Combine, and would rather wait for his pro-day. But competitiveness must have prevailed, because Johnson borrowed a pair of cleats, and recorded a 4.35 40 yard dash speed, a 42.5 inch vertical leap, and over an 11 and a half foot standing broad jump. Question answered. Crisis averted.

In addition to his explosive leaping ability, Megatron has an 82" wingspan, which combine to allow a maximum vertical reach, while airborne, of 12 and a half feet. This measurement of maximum vertical reach is higher than any NBA player has ever been officially measured.

Tight End

Vernon Davis had one of the most memorable combine performances ever, and managed to convert those athletic gifts into several Pro-Bowl selections. At 6'3" tall and 254 pounds, Davis ran the fastest 40 yard dash ever by a tight end, 4.38 seconds. He added 33 reps of 225 pounds on bench press (which extrapolates out to around a 450 lb max), and a 42 inch vertical leap as well. Vernon Davis is the fastest NFL prospects ever when 40 yard dash time is normalized to body weight, and he is the most explosive tight end in NFL history.

Offensive Tackle

Lane Johnson was a 6-foot-6, 220 pound all-state quarterback in high school, a state finalist in shot put, and a former quarterback and tight-end in junior college. Johnson bulked up to 250 pounds to play tight end in junior college, while maintaining 4.5-second speed. When Oklahoma recruited him as a tight-end, he continued to bulk up to 280 pounds until Bob Stoops ultimately moved the gifted athlete to offensive tackle. At the 2013 Combine, Lane John measured in at 6'6" tall and 303 pounds, and ran a

4.72 second 40 yard dash, becoming the second fastest offensive lineman in NFL Combine history.

Offensive Guard

The physical gifts of Bruce Campbell, former University of Maryland Terrapin and *Bruce Feldman: Workout Warrior* alumni, was no secret prior to the 2010 NFL Draft. Standing 6'6" and weighing 314 pounds, Campbell possessed a max bench press of 490 pounds (and 34 reps of 225 pounds) with extremely long arms, and nearly single digit body fat %. The prospective interior lineman could also move extraordinarily well, running a 4.85 40 yard dash (1.7-second 10 yard split), 32-inch vertical leap.

Center

Ryan Kalil has always been a master technician of the center position, but he is also vastly underrated as an athlete. On the field, he is a former 2-time National Champion and an All-American in college, an NFC Champion, a five-time pro-bowler, and a two-time All-Pro. His father was a former NFL Draft pick, and his brother is a former 4th overall Draft pick. Football is in his blood. And the man is extremely strong and fast. Ryan Kalil's 40 yard dash time of 4.96 seconds lands him in the 95th percentile of any center ever. Kalil also bench pressed 225 pounds for 34 reps, and ultimately was a second round pick in the 2007 NFL Draft.

Defensive Tackle

I could not choose just one player as the most athletic defensive tackle in NFL Combine history. Aaron Donald is arguably the best defensive player in the NFL right now, and appears to be a one-in-a-decade type talent at the position. But, his athletic gifts are not limited to playing football with pads on. Donald is also the fastest defensive tackle prospect ever with his 4.68 second time in the 40 Yard Dash. And, despite being small for a defensive tackle (6'1" 285 pounds), Donald managed to press 225 pounds 35 times and vertical leap 32 inches.

As astounding as Aaron Donald's athleticism is for his size, Dontari Poe is perhaps the freakiest big man ever. Poe bench pressed 225 pounds 44 times, which extrapolates out to an estimated max bench-press of over 520 pounds. Most people would struggle to do 44 push-ups. But, looking at Dontari Poe's frame, it isn't hard to believe that he is that strong. Weighing 345 pounds, Dontari Poe is the 8th heaviest defensive prospect ever. However…somehow he managed to still break the 5 second barrier in the 40 yard dash, running it in an unbelievable time of 4.98 seconds, which is one of the Top 10 fastest weight-normalized 40 yard dash times ever.

Defensive End

Mario Williams and J.J. Watt are not only perennial Pro-Bowlers. They are also responsible for two of the most impressive combine workouts in NFL history. Being such exceptional athletes, Williams and Watt played multiple sports and even multiple positions on the football field. Mario Williams played defensive end and running back in high school, and was a state qualifier in the shot put. J.J. Watt lettered in football, baseball, basketball, and won a state title in the shot put in track and field. Watt played wide receiver and defensive end in high school, tight end initially in college, and he still lines up as a tight end in the NFL. Despite Watt (6'5" 290 pounds) and Williams (6'7" 295 pounds) being two of the heavier defensive ends to ever workout at the Combine, they still rank unequivocally as the most athletically impressive ever. A video of J.J. Watt box-jumping 61 inches went viral and highlighted how unique Watt's athleticism (37 inch standing vertical leap) is for 290 pounds. Even more otherworldly, Mario Williams (6'7" 295 pounds) vertical leaped 40.5 inches, which is over 10 inches higher than the reining NBA MVP Oklahoma City Thunder's Russell Westbrook jumped at the NBA Combine.

Linebacker

Inside

Luke Kuechly had one of the most productive collegiate careers of any starting linebacker in the NFL. But heading into the 2012 NFL Combine, there were many questioning the highly productive Luke Kuechly's athleticism. In fact, many prominent media "scouts" labeled Keuchly as a sub-par athlete for the position. However, he quickly erased all doubt by turning in one of the greatest combine performances ever by an inside linebacker, and has since become an All-Pro for the Carolina Panthers. Kuechly ran a sub-4.6 second 40 yard dash, vertical leaped over 38 inches, and essentially led the linebacker class of 2012 in every combine metric.

Outside

Demarcus Ware is one of the most dominating pass rushers of this decade, and a newly crowned Super Bowl Champion. As a high school athlete, Demarcus Ware was thought to be undersized for a pass rusher in college. Despite the lack of bulk at the time, Ware was an incredibly explosive athlete. He could long-jump over 24 feet, high-jump well over 6 feet, and was voted Most Valuable Receiver on the football team. At Troy University, Ware transitioned to a full-time defensive player, and began bulking up his frame, registering outstanding numbers in the weight room: 430-pounds bench press, 570-pounds squat, and 360-pounds power clean. At the Combine, Ware showcased a rare combination of strength, size (260 pounds), elite speed (4.56-second 40 yard dash), and leaping ability (38.5 inch vertical), that led to him becoming the 20th overall pick in the 2005 NFL Draft.

Cornerback

Antonio Cromartie owns the NFL record for the longest return of any kind after returning a missed field goal 109 yards for a touchdown. So not surprisingly, he is a supremely gifted athlete. But, in my eyes, he is possibly the most athletic cornerback ever – including Deion Sanders (although he wasn't included in this dataset because his Combine was prior to 1999). A standout track and field athlete in probably the Nation's fastest state of Florida, Cromartie was a state finalist in high school for the 110 hurdles, 4 x 100 meter relay, and the triple jump. At Florida State, Cromartie was a member of the Seminoles' ACC Championship track and field team in 2004, running the 200 meters in 21.35 seconds and the 400 meter dash in

46.39 seconds. At the NFL Combine, the 6'2" Cromartie ran the 40 in 4.38 seconds, vertical leaped 42 inches, and broad jumped 11 feet.

Safety

Taylor Mays never had the NFL career that everyone expected from the enormous potential he showed in college. He was a 3-time First-team All American at USC, and universally known as an absolute physical freak in the weight room. But even before entering college, Taylor Mays was a generational talent in high school. He won Washington state titles in the 100 and 200 meter dash as a high school sophomore. Mays left the high school track to pursue football, but did not leave his speed behind. As a high school senior, Mays attended a Nike training camp where he ran a 4.59-second forty yard dash as a 218 pound safety prospect. Mays maintained a single-digit body fat percentage during his time at USC, but still managed to bulk up to 238 pounds before his senior year. At the 2010 NFL Combine, Mays ran a 4.43 second 40 yard dash and vertical leaped 41 inches while weighing 230 pounds.

Athlete

Before Matt Jones terrorized the SEC as a quarterback for the Arkansas Razorbacks, he was a multiple time All-State selection in football and basketball, and a McDonalds All-American in basketball. After only his junior year in high school, Jones broke the Arkansas high school basketball scoring record. Jones played one year for the Arkansas basketball team, and four years as the quarterback of the football team. Jones set the SEC record for career rushing yards by a QB and is perhaps the most unique athlete to ever perform at the NFL Combine. Standing 6-foot-6 and weighing 242 pounds, Jones had the frame of a defensive lineman, but ran a 4.37 in the forty yard dash, and vertical leaped 39.5 inches. Jones was drafted as a wide receiver by the Jacksonville Jaguars in the first round of the 2005 Draft, and had a relatively successful rookie year at a new position with 5 TD receptions. He battled personal problems during his NFL career, but was truly an exceptional and unique athlete.

Introducing Some Stats

The following chapters will begin introducing some statistical terms, which will get progressively more in depth. But if some of the terminology doesn't make sense or seems difficult to understand, don't get discouraged. These chapters will explore several different Combine datasets, and I will provide some examples of observing data from different statistical perspectives. Some of my conclusions or results will slightly change depending on the years included in the analysis, the analytical technique employed, or even the question that I'm exploring. I'm not aiming to convince you to accept any of the conclusions I present, I only hope that this helps you look at football just a little bit differently.

Who is the Fastest?

Of all the metrics and measurements collected at the NFL Scouting Combine, perhaps the most popular among fans, media and maybe even the players, is the 40 yard dash. Nearly everyone can remember racing as a child, and the bragging rights that came along with being the fastest kid in the neighborhood. Even at the summer Olympics, there is something undeniably exciting about the 100 meter dash, and finding out who the World's fastest man and woman are. This is no different in the NFL, where we all hear stories about legendary speedsters like Deion Sanders, Dennis Greene, Bob Hayes, and Bo Jackson. And the advent of the NFL Scouting Combine and the 40-yard dash only exacerbated the intrigue surrounding speed. But why 40 yards?

Legend has it that former coach Paul Brown coined the idea. Paul Brown was truly remarkable innovator. He's known as the first coach to use game film in scouting and hire a full-time staff of assistant coaches. He invented the face mask and played a major role is dissolving football's color barrier. And, he is credited with originating the timed 40 yard dash as a scouting tool. He choose the distance of 40 yards because he figured that 40 yards was roughly the average distance of a punt. Coach Brown also decided that that the average punt had approximately 4.5 seconds of hang time. So Brown surmised that if a player could run 40 yards in 4.5 seconds, he will be able to leave the line of scrimmage when a punt is kicked, and reach the point where the ball comes down just as it arrives. In the fifty years since, there have been many arguments over just how useful the 40 yard dash is as a scouting tool. But, we are just as fascinated by it as ever.

Following the 2015 NFL Combine, and just prior to the 2015 NFL Draft, I became interested in finding out who the fastest player in the Draft was. There were many prospects among the skill positions who ran a sub 4.3 second 40 yard dash. But I was also curious about the big guys who ran. Bodyweight undoubtedly has an effect on speed, so I needed a way to normalize or standardize 40 yard dash times to account for body weight. So, using a similar approach as Chase Stuart (a great football analytics writer) did in years' past, I used a linear regression to dissect the influence that bodyweight has on speed. I included approximately 2,400 combine participants dating back to 2003, and I performed a linear regression of body weight (pounds) vs 40 yard dash time (secs). This relationship is described by the following equation ($r^2 = 0.75$):

40 yard dash time (secs) = [0.006 x *body weight (pounds)*] + 3.309

And the figure below shows the plotted data with the regression line.

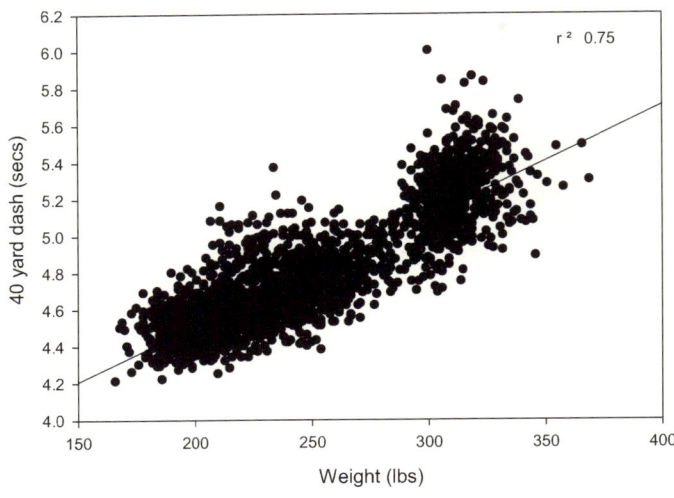

Weight (lbs) vs 40 yard dash (secs)

Note: For those not familiar with statistics… A linear regression basically draws a line, known as the *regression line*, through the middle of your data. If the data form a clear discernable pattern in one direction, then that is probably a strong relationship. If the data are randomly distributed around the line with no perceivable pattern at all, there is probably no statistical relationship. The term r^2 is a statistical measure of how close the data are to the fitted regression line. If the term $r^2 = 0.75$ for the plot of weight vs 40 yard dash time, you can essentially interpret that as: 75% of the variability in 40 yard dash time is explained by the weight of the prospect running.

So, digging deep into the 2015 Combine participants, I discovered that the fastest player at the 2015 NFL Combine was not one of the speedsters playing a skill position like Jamarcus Nelson, Trae Waynes, or Phillip Dorsett. Normalizing 40 yard dash time to body weight revealed that the 269 pound Alvin "Bud" Dupree was the fastest player at the 2015 Combine… and the second fastest (weight-normalized) defensive end prospect ever behind Mario Williams.

Given Bud Dupree's body weight of 269 pounds, he was predicted to run a 4.92 second 40 yard dash using the equation listed earlier. His actual 40 yard dash time of 4.56 seconds was approximately 0.36 seconds faster than expected, or predicted by that equation.

Year	Name	College	POS	Height (in)	Weight (lbs)	40 Yard Dash (secs)	Predicted 40 YD (secs)	40 YD Differential
2015	Alvin Dupree	Kentucky	DE	76	269	4.56	4.92	-0.36

Using this approach and the 2003-2015 Combine dataset, the fastest player in Combine history was determined to be Vernon Davis, who ran a full 0.45 seconds faster than what was expected of his 254 pound frame. The table below lists the 10 fastest weight normalized 40 yard dash times ever, which includes Davis, Calvin Johnson, Mario Williams, and "Bud" Dupree.

Year	Name	College	POS	Height (in)	Weight (lbs)	40 Yard Dash (secs)	Predicted 40 YD (secs)	40 YD Differential
2006	Vernon Davis	Maryland	TE	75	254	4.38	4.83	-0.45
2004	Tank Johnson	Washington	DT	75	304	4.69	5.13	-0.44
2013	Terron Armstead	Arkansas-Pine Bluff	OT	77	306	4.71	5.14	-0.43
2013	Lane Johnson	Oklahoma	OT	78	303	4.72	5.12	-0.40
2012	Dontari Poe	Memphis	DT	76	346	4.98	5.38	-0.40
2007	Calvin Johnson	Georgia Tech	WR	77	239	4.35	4.74	-0.39
2014	Greg Robinson	Auburn	OT	77	332	4.92	5.30	-0.38
2006	Mario Williams	North Carolina State	DE	79	295	4.70	5.08	-0.38
2011	Von Miller	Texas A&M	OLB	75	246	4.42	4.78	-0.36
2015	Alvin Dupree	Kentucky	DE	76	269	4.56	4.92	-0.36

Table 1: Fastest weight-normalized 40 yard dash times (2003-Present).

Of all the fastest weight-normalized 40 yard dash times in 2015, only Dupree was comparable to the fastest times of this decade. Dupree exceeded his expected time by 0.36 seconds, nearly a tenth of a second faster than anyone else in the 2015 class. The fastest weight-normalized 40 times from 2015 are listed in table 2.

Name	POS	College	Weight (lbs)	40 Yard Dash (secs)	Predicted 40 YD (secs)	40 YD Differential
Alvin Dupree	DE	Kentucky	269	4.56	4.92	-0.36
Owamagbe Odighizuwa	DE	UCLA	267	4.62	4.91	-0.29
Darren Waller	WR	Georgia Tech	238	4.46	4.73	-0.27
Dante Fowler Jr.	OLB	Florida	261	4.6	4.87	-0.27
Vic Beasley	OLB	Clemson	246	4.53	4.78	-0.25
Danielle Hunter	DE	LSU	252	4.57	4.82	-0.25
Kevin White	WR	West Virginia	215	4.35	4.60	-0.25
Dorial Green-Beckham	WR	Oklahoma	237	4.49	4.73	-0.24
Shane Ray	DE	Missouri	245	4.54	4.78	-0.24
Chris Conley	WR	Georgia	213	4.35	4.58	-0.23

Table 2: Fastest weight-normalized 40 yard dash times (2015).

Using the difference between predicted and actual 40 yard dash times (referred to as the *40 yard dash differential*), I compiled a list of the fastest players in the 2015 Draft Class which I call *The 2015 All-Speed Team*. This *Team* includes Heisman Trophy winner Marcus Mariota, Top 10 Draft pick Kevin White, Outland Trophy winner Brandon

Scherff, as well as All-Americans (and now All-Pros) Vic Beasley and Landon Collins.

Year	Name	POS	College	Weight (lbs)	40 Yard Dash (secs)	Predicted 40 Yard Dash (secs)	40 YD Differential
2015	Marcus Mariota	QB	Oregon	222	4.52	4.64	-0.12
2015	Karlos Williams	RB	Florida State	230	4.48	4.69	-0.21
2015	Darren Waller	WR	Georgia Tech	238	4.46	4.73	-0.27
2015	Kevin White	WR	West Virginia	215	4.35	4.60	-0.25
2015	MyCole Pruitt	TE	Southern Illinois	251	4.58	4.81	-0.23
2015	Brandon Scherff	OT	Iowa	319	5.05	5.22	-0.17
2015	Cedric OgbuehiInjured	OT	Texas A&M	306	4.98	5.14	-0.16
2015	Ali Marpet	OG	Hobart	307	4.98	5.15	-0.17
2015	Jarvis Harrison	OG	Texas A&M	330	5.19	5.29	-0.10
2015	Greg Mancz	C	Toledo	301	5.08	5.11	-0.03
2015	Xavier Cooper	DT	Washington State	293	4.86	5.06	-0.20
2015	Derrick Lott	DT	Chattanooga	314	4.99	5.19	-0.20
2015	Alvin Dupree	DE	Kentucky	269	4.56	4.92	-0.36
2015	Owamagbe Odighizuwa	DE	UCLA	267	4.62	4.91	-0.29
2015	Stephone Anthony	ILB	Clemson	243	4.56	4.76	-0.20
2015	Dante Fowler Jr.	OLB	Florida	261	4.6	4.87	-0.27
2015	Vic Beasley	OLB	Clemson	246	4.53	4.78	-0.25
2015	Trae Waynes	CB	Michigan State	186	4.31	4.42	-0.11
2015	Eric Rowe	CB	Utah	205	4.45	4.54	-0.09
2015	Justin Cox	FS	Mississippi State	191	4.36	4.45	-0.09
2015	Landon Collins	SS	Alabama	228	4.53	4.67	-0.14

Table 3: The 2015 All-Speed team from the NFL Combine.

When looking at how *The 2015 All-Speed Team* stacks up to *The All-Time Speed Team*, "Bud" Dupree was the only player included on both lists. I must point out that Dupree would have made the *All-Time Speed Team* as either a DE or OLB.

Year	Name	College	POS	Weight (lbs)	40 Yard Dash (secs)	Predicted 40 Yard Dash (secs)	40 YD Differential
2011	Cam Newton	Auburn	QB	248	4.56	4.79	-0.23
2005	Brandon Jacobs	Southern Illinois	RB	267	4.56	4.91	-0.35
2011	Mario Fannin	Auburn	RB	231	4.37	4.69	-0.32
2007	Calvin Johnson	Georgia Tech	WR	239	4.35	4.74	-0.39
2009	Darrius Heyward-Bey	Maryland	WR	210	4.25	4.57	-0.32
2006	Vernon Davis	Maryland	TE	254	4.38	4.83	-0.45
2013	Terron Armstead	Arkansas-Pine Bluff	OT	306	4.71	5.14	-0.43
2013	Lane Johnson	Oklahoma	OT	303	4.72	5.12	-0.40
2010	Marshall Newhouse	Texas Christian	OG	319	4.99	5.22	-0.23
2005	Evan Mathis	Alabama	OG	304	4.92	5.13	-0.21
2006	Chris Chester	Oklahoma	C	303	4.83	5.12	-0.29
2004	Tank Johnson	Washington	DT	304	4.69	5.13	-0.44
2012	Dontari Poe	Memphis	DT	346	4.98	5.38	-0.40
2006	Mario Williams	North Carolina State	DE	295	4.7	5.08	-0.38
2015	Alvin Dupree	Kentucky	DE	269	4.56	4.92	-0.36
2011	Martez Wilson	Illinois	ILB	250	4.49	4.81	-0.32
2011	Von Miller	Texas A&M	OLB	246	4.42	4.78	-0.36
2011	Dontay Moch	Nevada	OLB	248	4.44	4.79	-0.35
2010	Akwasi Owusu-Ansah	Indiana (PA)	CB	207	4.32	4.55	-0.23
2012	Josh Robinson	Central Florida	CB	199	4.29	4.50	-0.21
2009	Chris Clemons	Clemson	FS	208	4.33	4.56	-0.23
2008	Josh Barrett	Arizona State	SS	223	4.34	4.64	-0.30

Table 4: The All-Time All-Speed team from the NFL Combine.

During the 2015 NFL Scouting Combine, players like Vic Beasley and Dante Flower garnered much of the spotlight. However, Alvin "Bud" Dupree may have been the most impressive athlete there. Aside from his historically fast 40 yard dash, Dupree also recorded the 3rd highest vertical (42 inches) and 2nd highest broad jump (11'6") *ever* for his position (DL-LB), regardless of body-weight. A first team All-SEC pass rusher, Dupree is also one of the most explosive players to ever perform at the NFL Combine, and is possibly the most athletic player in the entire 2015 NFL Draft Class.

How Much Can You Bench?

How much can you bench? This is one of the go-to icebreakers amongst meatheads, and usually one of the first questions that come up when meeting a person who lifts weights. A strong bench press requires a well-balanced and muscled upper body. In bodybuilding circles, bench press is known as the principal chest exercise, but the movement also requires well-developed supporting muscularity surrounding the shoulder capsule, powerful triceps, and a strong upper back. Although the bench press was initially tested at the NFL Combine as a measure of upper-body muscular strength and endurance, there is now a nearly universal dismissal of its importance in NFL talent evaluation. A select few still believe the bench press holds merit as an indicator of work ethic, training discipline, or even raw strength. Regardless of the reason for intrigue…it is always fun to marvel at amazing feats of strength!

A previous study on 289 Division I football players exhibited that bench press reps with 225 pounds significantly correlated with one-rep-max in the bench press r=0.95, r²=0.90). This study derived the following equation that predicts one-rep max using the maximum number of repetitions with 225 pounds (Mann, Stoner, and Mayhew 2012).

One-Rep-Max Bench Press (pounds) = 221.8 pounds + (6.81 x Reps @ 225 pounds)

Using the equation above, I predicted bench press one-rep-max estimates for the strongest Combine participants overall and at each position from 1999 to 2015.

Year	Name	College	POS	Body Weight (lbs)	Bench Press Reps with 225 lbs	Estimated Bench Press Max (lbs)
1999	Justin Ernest	Eastern Kentucky	DT	281	51	569
2011	Stephen Paea	Oregon State	DT	303	49	555
2000	Leif Larsen	Texas-El Paso	DT	300	45	528
2010	Mitch Petrus	Arkansas	OG	310	45	528
2006	Mike Kudla	Ohio State	DE	265	45	528
2006	Brodrick Bunkley	Florida State	DT	306	44	521
2010	Jeff Owens	Georgia	DT	304	44	521
2012	Dontari Poe	Memphis	DT	346	44	521
2005	Scott Young	BYU	OG	312	43	515
2004	Isaac Sopoaga	Hawaii	DT	317	42	508
2014	Russell Bodine	North Carolina	OG	310	42	508
2007	Tank Tyler	North Carolina State	DT	306	42	508
2004	Igor Olshansky	Oregon	DT	315	41	501
2006	Terna Nande	Miami (OH)	OLB	232	41	501
2012	David Molk	Michigan	C	298	41	501
1999	Zach Piller	Florida	OT	331	40	494
2007	Justin Blalock	Texas	OG	320	40	494
2007	Manuel Ramirez	Texas Tech	OG	326	40	494

Justin Ernest still owns the NFL Combine record for bench press, with 51 reps of 225 pounds, but never managed to play a down in the league. Stephen Paea, an All-Pac 10 defensive tackle at Oregon State, came close to breaking the record in 2011, but fell 2 reps short. Since 1999, Ernest and Paea are the only two players with extrapolated one-rep-max presses of over 550 pounds. For comparative purposes, a 550 pound bench press would have beaten all but two super heavyweight raw powerlifters in the 2015 IPF World Powerlifting Championships. Former Baylor defensive tackle Andrew Billings broke the National High School Powerlifting record for total poundage lifted (805 pound squat, 500 pound bench, and 705 pound deadlift), but only managed 31 reps with 225 pounds, which correlates with an estimated 435 pound max. This Chapter was not meant to be an argument for the utility of the bench press in NFL talent evaluations. It was simply fun to look into. Whether or not you are a fan of the bench press, the forty yard dash, or even the vertical jump, these drills at the NFL Combine are simply fun to watch. For historical comparisons of bench press strength by position (1999 through 2015), check out the tables below.

Quarterback

Year	Name	College	Body Weight (lbs)	Bench Press Reps with 225 lbs	Bench Press Max (lbs)
2009	Jason Boltus	Hartwick	225	26	399
2009	Rhett Bomar	Sam Houston State (TX)	225	25	392
2007	Brady Quinn	Notre Dame	232	24	385
2006	Jay Cutler	Vanderbilt	226	23	378
2005	Adrian McPherson	Florida State	218	22	372

Running Back

Year	Name	College	Body Weight (lbs)	Bench Press Reps with 225 lbs	Bench Press Max (lbs)
2014	Jerick McKinnon	Georgia Southern	209	32	440
2013	Knile Davis	Arkansas	227	31	433
2011	Shane Vereen	California	210	31	433
2002	Rock Cartwright	Kansas State	237	30	426
2009	Rashad Jennings	Liberty	231	29	419

Wide Receiver

Year	Name	College	Body Weight (lbs)	Bench Press Reps with 225 lbs	Bench Press Max (lbs)
2011	Greg Little	North Carolina	231	27	406
2009	Brooks Foster	North Carolina	201	27	406
2013	T.J. Moe	Missouri	204	26	399
2008	Eddie Royal	Virginia Tech	184	24	385
2011	Niles Paul	Nebraska	224	24	385

Tight End

Year	Name	College	Body Weight (lbs)	Bench Press Reps with 225 lbs	Bench Press Max (lbs)
2014	Joe Don Duncan	Dixie State	268	35	460
2012	Orson Charles	Georgia	251	35	460
2007	Daniel Coats	BYU	257	34	453
2004	Ben Watson	Georgia	258	34	453
2006	Vernon Davis	Maryland	254	33	447

Offensive Tackle

Year	Name	College	Body Weight (lbs)	Bench Press Reps with 225 lbs	Bench Press Max (lbs)
1999	Zach Piller	Florida	331	40	494
2003	Tony Pashos	Illinois	337	38	481
2010	Russell Okung	Oklahoma State	307	38	481
2008	Jake Long	Michigan	313	37	474
2015	Ereck Flowers	Miami	329	37	474

Offensive Guard

Year	Name	College	Body Weight (lbs)	Bench Press Reps with 225 lbs	Bench Press Max (lbs)
2010	Mitch Petrus	Arkansas	310	45	528
2005	Scott Young	BYU	312	43	515
2014	Russell Bodine	North Carolina	310	42	508
2007	Justin Blalock	Texas	320	40	494
2007	Manuel Ramirez	Texas Tech	326	40	494

Center

Year	Name	College	Body Weight (lbs)	Bench Press Reps with 225 lbs	Bench Press Max (lbs)
2012	David Molk	Michigan	298	41	501
1999	Jeff Smith	Wyoming	286	38	481
1999	Craig Page	Georgia Tech	295	38	481
2001	Roberto Garza	Texas A&M-Kingsville	303	37	474
2002	Scott Peters	Arizona State	300	36	467

Defensive End

Year	Name	College	Body Weight (lbs)	Bench Press Reps with 225 lbs	Bench Press Max (lbs)
2006	Mike Kudla	Ohio State	265	45	528
2013	Margus Hunt	Southern Methodist	277	38	481
2008	Vernon Gholston	Ohio State	266	37	474
2013	Cornelius Washington	Georgia	265	36	467
2002	Ryan Denney	BYU	276	36	467

Defensive Tackle

Year	Name	College	Body Weight (lbs)	Bench Press Reps with 225 lbs	Bench Press Max (lbs)
1999	Justin Ernest	Eastern Kentucky	281	51	569
2011	Stephen Paea	Oregon State	303	49	555
2000	Leif Larsen	Texas-El Paso	300	45	528
2012	Dontari Poe	Memphis	346	44	521
2010	Jeff Owens	Georgia	304	44	521

Outside Linebacker

Year	Name	College	Body Weight (lbs)	Bench Press Reps with 225 lbs	Bench Press Max (lbs)
2006	Terna Nande	Miami (OH)	232	41	501
2012	Ronnell Lewis	Oklahoma	253	36	467
2015	Vic Beasley	Clemson	246	35	460
2005	Tyjuan Hagler	Cincinnati	236	35	460
2011	Bruce Miller	Central Florida	254	35	460

Inside Linebacker

Year	Name	College	Body Weight (lbs)	Bench Press Reps with 225 lbs	Bench Press Max (lbs)
2005	Liam Ezekiel	Northeastern	249	36	467
2010	Donald Butler	Washington	245	35	460
2004	Ryan Fowler	Duke	250	35	460
1999	Tony D'Amato	Utah State	240	34	453
2005	Robert McCune	Louisville	245	34	453

Cornerback

Year	Name	College	Body Weight (lbs)	Bench Press Reps with 225 lbs	Bench Press Max (lbs)
2007	Chris Houston	Arkansas	185	27	406
2015	Josh Shaw	Southern California	201	26	399
2011	Marcus Gilchrist	Clemson	195	26	399
2010	Kyle Wilson	Boise State	194	25	392
2009	Vontae Davis	Illinois	203	25	392

Free Safety

Year	Name	College	Body Weight (lbs)	Bench Press Reps with 225 lbs	Bench Press Max (lbs)
2002	Chris Hope	Florida State	210	28	412
2013	John Boyett	Oregon	204	27	406
2003	Derek Pagel	Iowa	208	25	392
2002	Kevin Curtis	Texas Tech	212	24	385
2010	Taylor Mays	Southern Californiaifornia	230	24	385

Strong Safety

Year	Name	College	Body Weight (lbs)	Bench Press Reps with 225 lbs	Bench Press Max (lbs)
2001	Adam Archuleta	Arizona State	211	31	433
2009	Jamarca Sanford	Mississippi	214	29	419
2013	Shamarko Thomas	Syracuse	213	28	412
2010	Lucien Antoine	Oklahoma State	215	28	412
2002	Coy Wire	Stanford	209	28	412

Jumping Out of Lucas Oil Stadium

In my opinion and based on my own research, the vertical leap is one of the more useful metrics from the NFL Combine. The vertical leap measures how explosive a prospect's lower body is, and potentially how well they can explode out of a stance. As Ted Sundquist and Brandon Thorn have explained in the past, the vertical leap is a *"very common athletic movement that occurs on a football field, albeit at various angles, and with pads on."* But, while the vertical jump has its importance in a talent evaluation, it is merely a small piece of the overall puzzle.

While most would assume that the world's greatest vertical jumpers play in the NBA, NFL prospects routinely outjump the best basketball players on the planet. At the NBA Combine, NBA prospects have their maximum vertical (with a running start) and no-step vertical leaps measured. The no-step vertical is the form measured at the NFL combine, and in my opinion, better equates to lower body explosion than a vertical leap with a running start.

Zach LaVine, back-to-back NBA Dunk Contest winner, and Aaron Gordon, 2016 Dunk Contest runner-up, recorded no-step vertical jumps of 33.5" and 32.5" respectively at the NBA Combine. In comparison, Mario Williams and J.J. Watt (both weighing over 290 pounds) outjumped LaVine, Gordon, and each of the NBA players listed in the Table below. Notable NBA players, and the highest vertical jumpers in NFL Combine history are shown in the two tables below.

Name	Height (in)	Weight (lbs)	No-Step Vertical Leap (in)	NBA Draft Pick Number
Damian Lillard	74	189	34.5	6
Zach LaVine	77	181	33.5	13
Victor Oladipo	75	213	33	2
Aaron Gordon	80	220	32.5	4
Blake Griffin	81	248	32	1
John Wall	75	196	30	1
Russell Westbrook	74	192	30	4
Stephen Curry	74	181	29.5	7
Derrick Williams	79	248	29	2
Evan Turner	78	214	27.5	2
Kawhi Leonard	78	227	25.5	15

Name	Height(in)	Weight(lbs)	Vertical Leap (in)	College	POS	Year
Gerald Sensabaugh	73	214	46	North Carolina	FS	2005
Cameron Wake	75	236	45.5	Penn State	OLB	2005
Chris McKenzie	69	185	45	Arizona State	CB	2005
Donald Washington	73	197	45	Ohio State	CB	2009
Chris Conley	74	213	45	Georgia	WR	2015
Chris Chambers	73	210	45	Wisconsin	WR	2001
Byron Jones	73	199	44.5	Connecticut	CB	2015
A.J. Jefferson	73	193	44	Fresno State	CB	2010
Dustin Fox	71	191	43.5	Ohio State	FS	2005
Jerry Azumah	70	195	43.5	New Hampshire	RB	1999

While NBA players are undoubtedly extraordinary leapers, the method of measurement for a vertical leap matters immensely. This is why I believe NFL talent evaluators could utilize the vast body of Strength and Conditioning research to better design meaningful metrics. Renowned coach and researcher Bret Contreras explained that vertical jumps, rapid changes of direction, and sprint "takeoffs" are among the most common motions in a variety of sports. Contreras suggested that the vertical leap has been used to assess these lower limb explosive capabilities because many studies demonstrate that vertical jumping ability is a good indicator of lower-limbs strength, power, and short sprint times.

NFL prospects are generally much more muscled and heavier than their NBA counterparts. But, leaping ability does appear to correlate with body weight (lower bodyweight ~ higher vertical jump, $r^2=0.41$). Like the linear regression I performed using body weight vs 40 yard dash time, I plotted vertical leap heights vs body weight for each NFL Combine participant from 1999-2015 (nflcombineresults.com). Using the equation below, I predicted vertical leaps for each Combine participant. Then, the predicted values were subtracted from the actual vertical leap measurements, and the differential *(+/- over Predicted)* was used to determine the best weight-normalized vertical jumper in combine history.

Vertical Leap (in) = 47.473 - (0.0597 x Body Weight (pounds))

Year	Name	College	POS	Height (in)	Weight (lbs)	Vertical Leap (in)	Predicted Vertical Leap (in)	(+ -) over Predicted
2005	Cameron Wake	Penn State	OLB	75	236	45.5	33.4	12.1
2005	Gerald Sensabaugh	North Carolina	FS	73	214	46	34.7	11.3
2006	Mario Williams	North Carolina State	DE	79	295	40.5	29.9	10.6
2015	Alvin Dupree	Kentucky	DE	76	269	42	31.4	10.6
2015	Chris Conley	Georgia	WR	74	213	45	34.8	10.2
2001	Chris Chambers	Wisconsin	WR	73	210	45	34.9	10.1
2011	Virgil Green	Nevada	TE	75	249	42.5	32.6	9.9
2015	Davis Tull	Tennessee-Chattanooga	OLB	74	246	42.5	32.8	9.7
2006	Vernon Davis	Maryland	TE	75	254	42	32.3	9.7
2006	Mark Anderson	Alabama	DE	76	254	42	32.3	9.7
2010	Dorin Dickerson	Pittsburgh	TE	74	226	43.5	34.0	9.5

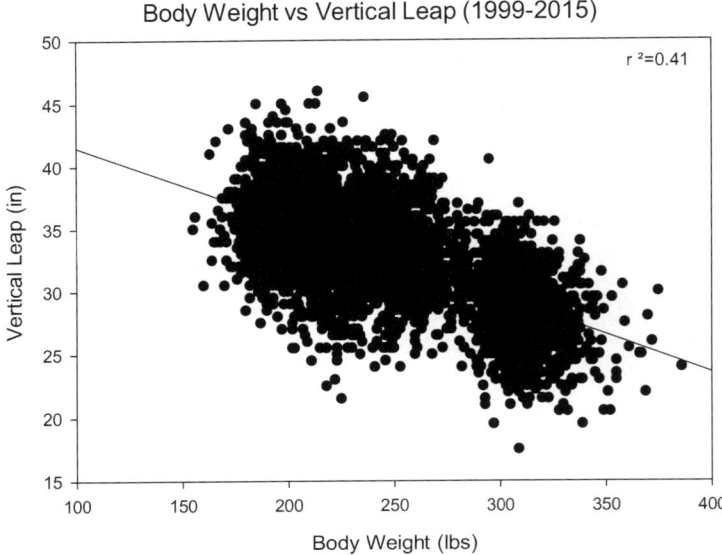

If you've seen the locker-room video clip of him snatching money from nearly 12 feet in the air, it should come as no surprise that All-Pro Defensive End Cameron Wake is an incredible athlete, and actually the best weight-normalized vertical jumper in combine history. Gerald Sensabaugh, Mario Williams, and Alvin "Bud" Dupree finish just behind Wake; all registered vertical leaps over 10" higher than what their body weight would predict.

For best vertical leaps by position (1999-2015), please see the tables below.

Quarterback

Year	Name	College	Height(in)	Weight(lbs)	Vertical Leap (in)
2011	Josh Portis	California (PA)	75	211	40
1999	Daunte Culpepper	Central Florida	76	255	39
2012	Robert Griffin	Baylor	74	223	39
2002	Josh McCown	Sam Houston State (TX)	76	223	38.5
2010	Tim Tebow	Florida	75	236	38.5

Running Back

Year	Name	College	Height(in)	Weight(lbs)	Vertical Leap (in)
1999	Jay Hinton	Morgan State (MD)	71	200	43.5
1999	Jerry Azumah	New Hampshire	70	195	43.5
2013	Christine Michael	Texas A&M	70	220	43
2015	Ameer Abdullah	Nebraska	69	205	42.5
2002	William Green	Boston College	73	221	42

Wide Receiver

Year	Name	College	Height(in)	Weight(lbs)	Vertical Leap (in)
2001	Chris Chambers	Wisconsin	73	210	45
2015	Chris Conley	Georgia	74	213	45
2001	Kevin Kasper	Iowa	73	199	43.5
2012	Kashif Moore	Connecticut	69	180	43.5
2001	Cedric James	Texas Christian	74	204	43

Tight End

Year	Name	College	Height(in)	Weight(lbs)	Vertical Leap (in)
2010	Dorin Dickerson	Pittsburgh	74	226	43.5
2011	Virgil Green	Nevada	75	249	42.5
2006	Vernon Davis	Maryland	75	254	42
2009	Jared Cook	South Carolina	77	246	41
2003	Visanthe Shiancoe	Morgan State (MD)	77	251	39.5

Offensive Tackle

Year	Name	College	Height(in)	Weight(lbs)	Vertical Leap (in)
2003	Kwame Harris	Stanford	79	310	35.5
2012	Donald Stephenson	Oklahoma	78	312	35.5
2005	Alex Barron	Florida State	80	318	35.5
2009	Lydon Murtha	Nebraska	79	306	35
2003	Jon Stinchcomb	Georgia	77	302	35

Offensive Guard

Year	Name	College	Height(in)	Weight(lbs)	Vertical Leap (in)
2005	Leon Robinson	Georgia Tech	76	314	36
2003	Eric Steinbach	Iowa	78	297	36
2005	Evan Mathis	Alabama	77	304	35.5
2009	Travis Bright	BYU	76	321	35.5
2001	Mathias Nkwenti	Temple	76	293	35.5

Center

Year	Name	College	Height(in)	Weight(lbs)	Vertical Leap (in)
2002	Ben Miller	Air Force	75	263	37.5
2001	Casey Rabach	Wisconsin	77	298	34.5
2005	Rob Hunt	North Dakota State	76	301	34.5
2004	Nick Hardwick	Purdue	76	295	34
2000	Brad Meester	Northern Iowa	76	298	34

Defensive End

Year	Name	College	Height(in)	Weight(lbs)	Vertical Leap (in)
2006	Mark Anderson	Alabama	76	254	42
2015	Alvin Dupree	Kentucky	76	269	42
2001	Reggie Hayward	Iowa State	77	255	41
2007	Brian Robison	Texas	75	259	40.5
2006	Mario Williams	North Carolina State	79	295	40.5

Defensive Tackle

Year	Name	College	Height(in)	Weight(lbs)	Vertical Leap (in)
2010	Al Woods	Louisiana State	76	309	37
2000	Al Lucas	Troy	73	294	36
2012	J.R. Sweezy	North Carolina State	77	298	36
2010	Ndamukong Suh	Nebraska	76	307	35.5
2005	Lynn McGruder	Oklahoma	74	303	35.5

Outside Linebacker

Year	Name	College	Height(in)	Weight(lbs)	Vertical Leap (in)
2005	Cameron Wake	Penn State	75	236	45.5
2015	Davis Tull	Tennessee-Chattanooga	74	246	42.5
2002	Scott Fujita	California	78	248	42
2003	Boss Bailey	Georgia	75	233	42
2011	Dontay Moch	Nevada	73	248	42

Inside Linebacker

Year	Name	College	Height(in)	Weight(lbs)	Vertical Leap (in)
2015	Benardrick McKinney	Mississippi State	76	246	40.5
2002	Tyreo Harrison	Notre Dame	74	238	40
2010	Jason Beauchamp	UNLV	75	244	39.5
2012	Mychal Kendricks	California	71	239	39.5
2007	Patrick Willis	Mississippi	73	242	39

Cornerback

Year	Name	College	Height(in)	Weight(lbs)	Vertical Leap (in)
2009	Donald Washington	Ohio State	73	197	45
2005	Chris McKenzie	Arizona State	69	185	45
2015	Byron Jones	Connecticut	73	199	44.5
2010	A.J. Jefferson	Fresno State	73	193	44
2009	Darius Butler	Connecticut	71	183	43

Free Safety

Year	Name	College	Height(in)	Weight(lbs)	Vertical Leap (in)
2005	Gerald Sensabaugh	North Carolina	73	214	46
2005	Dustin Fox	Ohio State	71	191	43.5
2010	Eric Berry	Tennessee	73	211	43
2005	Kerry Rhodes	Louisville	75	209	42
1999	Pierson Prioleau	Virginia Tech	70	191	42

Strong Safety

Year	Name	College	Height(in)	Weight(lbs)	Vertical Leap (in)
2001	Jarrod Cooper	Kansas State	73	222	41.5
2004	Bob Sanders	Iowa	69	204	41.5
2002	Wesly Mallard	Oregon	74	221	41
2000	Tyrone Carter	Minnesota	68	190	41
2006	Michael Huff	Texas	73	204	40.5

The NFL Combine: What Does History Tell Us?

According to some NFL personnel, the most useful aspects of the NFL Scouting Combine are the medical assessments and the interviews. However, it does offer a chance for scouts to time and measure prospects in the same controlled setting and compile a data repository. It is difficult to draw conclusions about a prospect's potential solely from their performance at the NFL Combine because of the multitude of other unaccounted-for variables including an athlete's actual ability to play football, intelligence, character, and other intangibles. For example, just because an athlete is extremely fast in one direction does not necessarily translate to fluidity, spatial awareness, hand-eye coordination, or competiveness. But, the NFL Combine does offer a very important service similar to what the SAT, GRE, or MCAT offer academic institutions.

Standardized tests are often criticized, and sometimes rightfully so, but they do exactly what they are meant to do: standardize. In undergraduate and graduate school applications, the SAT, GRE, or MCAT are meant to compare candidates from different schools or backgrounds while holding all other variables constant. Should you choose your surgeon based solely on his MCAT scores? No. A proven track record, recommendations, commitment to one's craft, and character are all very important attributes that are not measured by a standardized test. But, GRE or MCAT scores are used in the application process because schools recognize that, statistically, students below a specific threshold of testing performance, do not perform well at that particular school. There are always exceptions to the rule. The same logic applies to comparing NFL draft prospects based on standardized tests of athleticism.

While the NFL Combine was originally organized to allow better comparisons of prospects in each draft class, it also allows for comparisons across different draft classes. Assuming that these drills are performed and measured exactly the same each year, Combine data should be comparable across different years. So, having Combine data for each prospect over time, and NFL data describing how well these prospects performed in the NFL (i.e QBR, sacks, Approximate Value, etc.), one could theoretically identify what Combine measurements, if any, are important for predicting NFL potential for each position. One way to approach this is similar to the way academic institutions grade standardized tests: percentile based or probability ranked.

In an attempt to isolate which athletic attributes were important for NFL success at each position, I decided to rank each NFL prospect's Combine measurements at each position. To do this, I assigned a percentile rank to each prospect for a given position. This dataset includes 15 years of Combine data (1999-2014), so players are ranked historically by position. For instance, Chris Johnson's 40 yard dash time of 4.24 will rank in the 99th percentile for running backs, while Vernon Davis' 40 yard dash time of 4.38 will also rank in the 99th percentile for tight ends.

To assign a percentile rank (aka known as a probability rank), I used a Weibull Rank formula (This is not very important to the majority of readers, but I wanted to make note of it. In probability theory within the field of statistics, the Weibull distribution is a continuous probability distribution. So I simply calculated a given probability rank, or percentile rank, for each prospect using this formula. Again, not crucially important).

So, using that methodology, I Weibull ranked NFL Draft prospects' height, weight, 40 yard dash time, bench press, vertical leap, broad jump, short shuttle run time, and 3 cone drill time for each position. Each Weibull rank was based on the sample size of the position group: 121 offensive tackles, 90 offensive guards, 42 centers, 105 running backs, 190 wide receivers, 104 tight ends, 92 defensive tackles, 107 defensive ends, 129 linebackers, 158 cornerbacks, and 108 safeties over the last 15 years. Only players who have played or started in at least 5 NFL games were included this dataset. I then calculated a mean rank, or average rank, for each prospect's rank in a given Combine drill or test. I originally wanted to perform a multiple linear regression of "Average Combine Rank vs NFL Career Approximate Value (Career AV)" to elucidate if one could predict value solely based on a cumulative metric from the Combine.

> Note: Career Approximate Value (CarAV) is a metric derived by Doug Drinen from Pro-Football Reference. CarAV is a single number representing the value of a player at any position from any year in the NFL. More information can be found at pro-football-reference.com.

When performing the regression of average rank vs career approximate value (CarAV) for each player in the NFL, I noticed that every category was not necessarily important.

For instance, a high percentile ranking in height for a running back does not translate into any logical or statistical advantage in the NFL. Therefore, I created several indices to the more meaningful metrics for each position. These indices are explained below:

Average Cumulative Rank (All measurements: height, weight, 40 yard dash, bench press, vertical leap, broad jump, short shuttle run, and 3 cone drill)

Explosive Index (40 yard dash, vertical leap, and broad jump)

Movement Index (40 yard dash, shuttle run, and 3 cone drill)

Force Index (Bench press and vertical leap)

Length Index (Height, vertical leap, and broad jump)

Running Back Index (Weight, 40 yard dash, vertical leap, and 3 cone drill)

The Explosive Index aims to capture explosiveness in one direction. The Movement Index is meant to represent how well a prospect moves linearly and laterally. The Force Index seems ideal for capturing a defensive tackle prospect's upper and lower body explosion because it includes only the bench press and vertical leap. The Running Back Index attempts to represent attributes of a successful running back: mass, speed, lower body explosion, and agility.

The correlative power of combine measurements has routinely been proven quite worthless in definitely predicting NFL success. But, I've only ever seen reports on the predictive strength of these predictive models using the mean response, or response of the 50th percentile in the distribution. For instance, a linear model of vertical leap vs CarAV may not be statically significant, or even visually interesting. However, when looking at response of the population (and the R^2 values) at varying quantiles (or percentiles of the distribution), we see that some of these Combine metrics, and the indices I calculated, are interesting. These indices are clearly not definitive, and possibly not even worth mentioning in a final scouting report. But, this aggregate ranking approach to interpreting Combine data may be a worthwhile alternative to more simplistic comparisons. In fact, some of these indices are explaining more than 20% of the variance between prospects' Career Approximate Value. For example, the Average Cumulative Rank for defensive ends shows no relationship at the typically reported 50th quantile. But, when looking at the 75th and 95th quantiles, 10% and 14% of the variance in Defensive End CarAV is explained using Average Cumulative Rank as a predictor.

I like to think of raw athleticism (i.e. sprinting speed, leaping ability, physical strength, etc) as a proverbial ceiling to potential. An NFL player's innate athleticism may cap how good that player will become, but it doesn't mean a player won't be productive. It potentially can determine whether a running back plays all three downs and becomes an All-Pro, but it may not prevent a player from rushing for 1000 yards. Using raw athleticism logically and statistically appears much more appropriate for projecting maximum potential (higher quantiles) rather than average production (typical mean or median response reported by linear models). The table below shows how strong correlations are between athleticism and CarAV at different percentiles of the population. The R^2 of 0.80 suggests that using the Running Back Index as a predictor for CarAV only appears to be relevant for predicting maximum potential (i.e. how well the 95th percentile performs).

Position	Predictor Index Used	R^2 50th quantile	75th quantile	95th quantile
OT	Explosive	0.06	0.07	0.04
OG	Explosive	0.05	0.09	0.06
C	Explosive	0.02	0.05	0.04
RB	Running Back	0.07	0.02	0.80
WR	Movement	0.19	0.05	0.05
TE	Cumulative	0.16	0.24	0.01
DT	Force	0.04	0.00	0.07
DT	Cumulative	0.00	0.08	0.69
DE	Cumulative	0.01	0.10	0.14
LB	Cumulative	0.05	0.07	0.33
CB	Length	0.16	0.03	0.00
S	Explosive	0.28	0.16	0.03

Statistically, these indices offer an interesting, but incomplete insight into athletic potential at different positions on the field. The tables below show the top 10 scoring athletes for each position at their most important respective index. For example, offensive tackles were best correlated with the Explosive Index. Which, logically, I can understand. There is a huge demand for large, highly athletic men at offensive tackle to protect quarterbacks, as illustrated by Michael Lewis' *The Blind Side*. This is not to suggest that a high grade in the Explosive Index absolutely correlates to NFL success. But we do see many of the most successful tackles in this dataset registering the highest Explosive Index scores.

Offensive Tackles

Year	Name	College	CarAV	Games Played	Games Started	Explosive Index
2010	Trent Williams	Oklahoma	31	60	59	96.99
2003	Jon Stinchcomb	Georgia	44	90	80	96.45
2007	Joe Thomas	Wisconsin	59	115	115	91.53
2004	Jake Scott	Idaho	58	131	128	89.89
2004	Adrian Jones	Kansas	12	55	26	89.34
2010	Jared Veldheer	Hillsdale	22	56	51	88.52
2003	Jordan Gross	Utah	73	167	167	88.25
2006	Daryn Colledge	Boise State	52	132	128	87.98
2005	Khalif Barnes	Washington	44	127	107	87.43
2003	Wade Smith	Memphis	42	141	98	84.70

Offensive Guards and Centers are not as well known for athleticism as tackles, but like the Tackles, the Explosive Index was the most significant predictor of all the indices. Many of the most explosive Guards and Centers have been very successful in the NFL, including Steve Hutchinson, Chris Snee, Nick Hardwick, Nick Mangold, and Ryan Khalil.

Offensive Guards

Year	Name	College	CarAV	Games played	Games Started	Explosive Index
2005	Evan Mathis	Alabama	19	63	43	98.17
1999	Cameron Spikes	Texas A&M	13	63	30	94.51
2010	Shelley Smith	Colorado State	5	31	12	93.77
2005	Scott Young	BYU	59	133	122	91.94
2004	Justin Smiley	Alabama	30	88	78	87.91
2001	Dennis Norman	Princeton	10	45	23	81.68
2001	Steve Hutchinson	Michigan	95	169	169	79.12
2006	Chris Kuper	North Dakota	33	90	79	78.39
2003	Vince Manuwai	Hawaii	45	111	105	77.66
2004	Chris Snee	Boston College	75	141	141	73.26

Centers

Year	Name	College	CarAV	Games played	Games Started	Explosive Index
2000	Brad Meester	Northern Iowa	83	194	193	90.70
2006	Chris Chester	Oklahoma	41	125	99	86.82
2002	Seth McKinney	Texas A&M	21	93	46	86.05
2001	Dominic Raiola	Nebraska	63	208	192	85.27
2004	Nick Hardwick	Purdue	68	136	136	80.62
2005	Eric Ghiaciuc	Central Michigan	19	48	42	79.07
2005	Chris Spencer	Mississippi	37	128	90	68.99
2006	Nick Mangold	Ohio State	64	130	130	65.89
2007	Ryan Kalil	Southern California	45	90	88	61.24
2012	A.Q. Shipley	Penn State	8	34	18	59.69

The Running Back (RB) Index did seem somewhat valuable in identifying successful backs in the NFL. Tomlinson and Peterson are arguably the best backs of this generation. Backs like Doug Martin and Ryan Mathews have both had impressive years as well.

Running Backs

Year	Name	College	CarAV	Games played	Games Started	RB Index
2011	Roy Helu	Nebraska	9	38	5	80.66
2010	Ben Tate	Auburn	13	41	10	80.42
2001	LaDainian Tomlinson	TCU	129	170	155	79.48
2010	Montario Hardesty	Tennessee	4	24	5	77.59
2012	Doug Martin	Boise St.	17	24	24	75.24
2010	Toby Gerhart	Stanford	13	65	10	71.70
2011	Mikel Leshoure	Illinois	5	17	14	71.23
2006	Jerious Norwood	Mississippi St.	20	66	6	70.05
2007	Adrian Peterson	Oklahoma	76	104	97	66.75
2005	J.J. Arrington	California	11	58	8	66.51
2010	Ryan Mathews	Fresno St.	35	56	47	64.86

Wide Receivers were by far the most difficult class to predict using Combine data. When scouting receivers, standardized combine drills are most likely far less important than analyzing route running skill, film study, and collegiate production.

Wide Receivers

Year	Name	College	CarAV	Games played	Games Started	Movement Index
2002	Tim Carter	Auburn	9	71	11	73.68
2001	Kevin Kasper	Iowa	2	39	9	70.18
2009	Tiquan Underwood	Rutgers	9	45	10	61.40
2010	Emmanuel Sanders	SMU	16	59	21	49.12
2003	Kevin Curtis	Utah State	26	81	36	40.35
2007	Anthony Gonzalez	Ohio State	16	40	12	50.88
2008	Andre Caldwell	Florida	12	78	16	42.11
2002	Deion Branch	Louisville	52	140	111	49.12
2002	Javon Walker	Florida State	39	83	46	36.84
2009	Johnny Knox	Abilene Christian	19	45	27	42.11

Tight Ends were an interesting position class to analyze because all the Combine measurements used in the predictions appeared to be statistically important. Over the past few decades, the NFL has been dominated by athletic freaks at Tight End like Tony Gonzalez, Rob Gronkowski, Jimmy Graham, and Antonio Gates. Gronkowski and Gates were not used in this study due to a lack of data. But, the top three physical freaks in this dataset based on an aggregate of all Combine measurables were Jordan Cameron, Jimmy Graham, and Vernon Davis. Jordan Cameron was a Pro Bowl selection in 2013, while Graham and Davis are multiple time Pro Bowlers and former All Pro selections.

Tight Ends

Year	Name	College	CarAV	Games played	Games Started	Average Cumulative Rank
2011	Jordan Cameron	Southern California	8	39	24	76.55
2010	Jimmy Graham	Miami	33	66	40	74.76
2006	Vernon Davis	Maryland	41	122	120	74.64
2012	James Hanna	Oklahoma	2	36	13	74.40
2003	L.J. Smith	Rutgers	21	98	65	71.79
1999	Dan Campbell	Texas A&M	6	106	71	70.24
2003	Visanthe Shiancoe	Morgan State (MD)	23	149	89	68.57
2008	Dustin Keller	Purdue	23	72	48	68.45
2004	Ben Watson	Georgia	31	135	98	68.21
2011	Rob Housler	Florida Atlantic	7	42	23	65.95

Defensive Tackles are often scouted as either quick gap penetrators or massive players that can take up space and command double teams. For this reason, I used both the Force Index (which includes the bench press and vertical leap), and the Average Cumulative Rank (all Combine measurements). The top 3 scores in the Force Index have all made All Pro teams in the NFL: Haloti Ngata, Dontari Poe, and B.J. Raji. The Average Rank for defensive tackles was not as correlative as the Force Index, but it was interesting seeing that All-Pros Geno Atkins and Ndamukong Suh were ranked in the top 5.

Defensive Tackles

Year	Name	College	CarAV	Games played	Games Started	Force Index
2006	Haloti Ngata	Oregon	88	127	124	86.02
2012	Dontari Poe	Memphis	18	34	34	80.29
2009	B.J. Raji	Boston College	28	76	63	79.21
2004	Isaac Sopoaga	Hawaii	39	139	89	78.49
2010	Linval Joseph	East Carolina	21	56	49	77.06

Year	Name	College	CarAV	Games played	Games Started	Average Cumulative Rank
2012	Kendall Reyes	Connecticut	10	35	23	73.52
2012	Derek Wolfe	Cincinnati	13	30	30	71.24
2006	Barry Cofield	Northwestern	42	128	127	71.10
2010	Geno Atkins	Georgia	38	60	44	68.68
2010	Ndamukong Suh	Nebraska	41	65	65	68.68

Defensive Ends, like Tight Ends, seem to be dominated by athletic freaks. The Average Cumulative Rank was the best predictor for Defensive End success in the NFL. Mario Williams and J.J. Watt top the list here.

Defensive Ends

Year	Name	College	CarAV	Games played	Games Started	Average Cumulative Rank
2006	Mario Williams	North Carolina State	54	118	118	82.06
2011	J.J. Watt	Wisconsin	40	52	52	80.21
2004	Travis LaBoy	Hawaii	22	95	46	72.45
2009	Michael Johnson	Georgia Tech	29	82	47	71.41
2010	Daniel Teo-Nesheim	Washington	11	39	27	70.60
2001	Kyle Vanden Bosch	Nebraska	62	152	137	70.02
2007	Chris Gocong	Cal Poly	31	79	67	68.52
2008	Vernon Gholston	Ohio State	6	45	5	67.36
2007	Adam Carriker	Nebraska	22	65	58	67.25
2007	Brian Robison	Texas	26	114	58	67.13

Outside and inside linebackers in the NFL were also dominated by players with the highest Average Ranks across all Combine drills. Demarcus Ware, Von Miller, Luke Kuechly, and Justin Houston are All-Pros. Brian

Cushing, Jamie Collins, and A.J. Hawk have all been very productive in the NFL as well.

Linebackers

Year	Name	College	CarAV	Games played	Games Started	Average Cumulative Rank
2005	DeMarcus Ware	Troy	88	144	143	86.25
2011	Von Miller	Texas A&M	33	43	43	78.85
2012	Luke Kuechly	Boston College	22	35	35	76.73
2011	Justin Houston	Georgia	23	46	40	74.23
2009	Brian Cushing	Southern California	34	59	59	70.29
2006	Jon Alston	Stanford	5	39	8	68.75
2013	Jamie Collins	Southern Mississippi	5	18	10	67.69
2007	Quincy Black	New Mexico	19	81	40	67.60
2005	Darryl Blackstock	Virginia	6	74	7	66.73
2006	A.J. Hawk	Ohio State	53	129	126	66.44

Cornerbacks are perhaps the most athletic players in the NFL. But, despite what many would think, cornerback value in the NFL was difficult to predict when only accounting for speed and quickness. However, players with the highest Length Index (which incorporates a player's height, vertical leap, and broad jump), generally have high Career Approximate Value as well. Among the players with high ranks in the Length Index, Richard Sherman and Charles Tillman are multiple time Pro Bowlers and former All-Pro selections. Dominique Rodgers-Cromartie, Aqib Talib, and Terrance Newman have all had very good careers as well.

Cornerbacks

Year	Player	College	CarAV	Games played	Games Started	Length Index
2008	Dominique Rodgers-Cromartie	Tennessee St.	30	96	79	87.63
2010	Chris Cook	Virginia	8	37	29	86.58
2006	Will Blackmon	Boston Col.	8	62	11	84.49
2003	Charles Tillman	La-Lafayette	69	156	152	80.92
2005	Stanford Routt	Houston	23	119	60	78.83
2011	Richard Sherman	Stanford	37	51	45	77.36
2008	Aqib Talib	Kansas	31	80	66	75.26
2009	Darius Butler	Connecticut	15	73	26	75.05
2005	Carlos Rogers	Auburn	47	130	120	74.84
2003	Terence Newman	Kansas St.	64	164	162	74.21

The Explosive Index appeared to correlate fairly well with successful NFL safeties. Eric Berry is an All-Pro for the Chiefs, while Bob Sanders had a brief but very exciting career for the Colts.

Safeties

Year	Player	College	CarAV	Games played	Games Started	Explosive Index
2010	Eric Berry	Tennessee	25	50	50	94.77
2004	Bob Sanders	Iowa	33	50	48	93.46
2006	Jason Allen	Tennessee	13	98	23	90.85
2013	Eric Reid	LSU	9	20	20	82.03
2009	Chris Clemons	Clemson	19	72	48	82.03
2003	Terrence Kiel	Texas A&M	20	59	51	79.41
2002	Tank Williams	Stanford	20	70	59	78.76
2006	Ko Simpson	South Carolina	14	41	32	78.43
2002	Jon McGraw	Kansas St.	18	122	36	78.10
2006	Daniel Bullocks	Nebraska	7	31	22	77.45

Statistically, using probabilistic indices is an interesting tool for investigating important athletic indicators at different positions. The NFL Combine does a great job of standardizing drills and measurements. Using state-of-the-art video and laser timing has helped tremendously in record keeping. And because of this technology, yearly or historical comparisons can offer valuable insight on potential similarities between a prospect and current or former players in the NFL. And, just as you would not award an undergraduate student with a high MCAT score an M.D. degree; players should not be drafted solely on combine measurements.

Integrating skills from other scientific disciplines

***

The next few chapters will delve into deeper quantitative analysis of NFL Combine data. I aim to present several examples of borrowing skills or analytical approaches from other scientific disciplines. As you read, keep in mind that the overarching question basically remains the same: *Does the NFL Combine matter in NFL talent evaluations?* But remember, the purpose of this book is to present different ways of analyzing that rather simple question.

The physiology behind the NFL Combine

The 40 yard dash is a measure of linear speed of an athlete. It requires a tremendous amount of quadriceps and glute power at the start, and foot speed, fluidity, and hamstring power through the drive phase and finish. Many challenge the utility of the 40 yard dash because football players rarely run 40 yards in a straight line. However, it is a metric of linear speed, acceleration, and explosiveness. Linear athleticism is arguably an extremely valuable attribute in football. For instance, a wide receiver or running back's ability to accelerate downfield is pertinent to competing. Other positions, like a linebacker for instance, may benefit more from lateral quickness than linear speed alone. And in reality, playing football requires a multitude of different athletic attributes. Some of these skills are easily measured, and some are not. And still, some athletic attributes necessary to play football at the highest level have yet to be translated to into a measureable test that can be implemented at the NFL Scouting Combine.

The 20 yard short shuttle (often referred to as simply the *shuttle run*) is a measure of an athlete's multidirectional quickness and agility. The shuttle run tests an athlete's ability to accelerate, decelerate, and rapidly accelerate again. The ability to start-and-stop, and change directions is very important in football. The shuttle run requires tremendous eccentric power throughout an athlete's hips, thighs, and glutes, as well as coordination throughout the body which is usually dependent on a powerful and sturdy core. The shuttle run is thought of as a metric of lateral power and speed, as opposed to the linear nature of the 40 yard dash. Changing direction explosively is undoubtedly necessary to play football at a high level.

The 3-cone drill is a bit more complex than most of the other combine drills. The 3-cone drill tests the ability of an athlete to accelerate, stop, and explode again. It also requires the athlete to drop their hips, turn around a corner, and accelerate out of that turn. An athlete needs a tremendous amount of balance while accelerating. The athlete must have powerful hips, thighs, and core, and also possess great flexibility in the hip, knee, and ankles to perform well in this drill. Defensive ends often need to accelerate around "the corner" (the edge of a pocket set by an offensive tackle) when pass rushing. A kick returner or even open field runner must retain acceleration while bouncing a return or run around blockers. Therefore, the 3-cone drill may serve as a surrogate for such necessary but multilayered athleticism.

The vertical leap is a test of both anterior and posterior chain explosiveness. At its core, it measures an athlete's ability to generate instant vertical power. A more detailed description of the vertical leap has been mentioned earlier in this book, and discussed at length in the *Power Output and Pass Rushing* Chapter.

The relatively small number of academic studies on the NFL Combine have largely reported that NFL Combine metrics offer no significant capabilities in predicting on-field performance in the NFL. The lack of success in

Combine metrics as a predictive tool is probably due to many reasons. There is most likely a substantial amount of *noise* (or variability) in Combine data sets, and NFL success is highly variable due to *everything* else that cannot be measured at the Combine.

How can the combine predict NFL potential?

A fascinating study by Kevin Meers, now an analyst for the Cleveland Browns, suggested that most of the measurements taken at the NFL Combine do a poor job at predicting NFL production. To briefly summarize some of Meers's findings:

- The vertical leap, broad jump, and 3-cone drill do not accurately predict production for any offensive position on the field.
- Bench press was only a significant predictor for tight ends
- Height was negatively correlated with running back success
- Short shuttle was significant for centers, while weight was important for running backs and offensive tackles.
- The 40 yard dash was a significant predictor for running backs, tight ends, guards, and offensive tackles.
- On the defensive side of the ball, the 3-cone drill did a much better job of predicting than on the offensive side.

Overall, Meers concluded that his NFL Combine multiple regressions did quite little to explain the success of NFL prospects.

Like Meers, I also wanted to explore the relationship between players' value in the league, and their performances at the NFL Scouting Combine. I hypothesized that the value in these Combine metrics would vary based on the particular athletic needs of the position. For instance, maybe success in the NFL at wide receiver would require a fast 40 yard dash time, whereas a successful NFL defensive end would preferentially require agility as measured by the 3-cone drill.

To do this, I investigated correlations between Career Approximate Value (CarAV - a metric created by Doug Drinen of Pro Football Reference), and a prospect's performance in four combine drills: the 40 yard dash, the vertical leap, the 20 yard shuttle run, and the 3-cone drill. I examined NFL prospects from 1999 to 2013 from all positions excluding QBs, kickers, and punters. My sample sizes for each position were as follows 121 offensive tackles, 90 offensive guards, 42 centers, 105 running backs, 190 wide receivers, 104 tight ends, 92 defensive tackles, 107 defensive ends, 129 linebackers, 158 cornerbacks, and 108 safeties. I used an analytical technique called Quantile Regression.

> Note: This is a detailed explanation of Quantile Regression. It isn't necessary to understand some of the conclusions from this study, but you may find it interesting and/or informative.

Quantile regression is a technique to estimate the quantiles of a response variable distribution in a linear model. Quantiles are essentially percentiles, so data at the 0.5 quantile are equal to the 50th percentile. Simple linear regressions only report an r^2 for the median quantile, or 50th percentile. This is why a line is drawn directly through the center of a regression. However, looking at other quantiles may provide a more complete view of possible relationships between the predictor and response variables. An NFL draft prospect evaluation typically includes a number of different statistics and measurements, but still there are countless others not quantified or reported. Consequently, there generally appears to be weak or no significant linear relationships between collegiate production or Combine metrics and future NFL production. By looking only at the median quantile response, quantitative models may be overlooking very meaningful relationships between those predictor stats/numbers and a prospect's NFL success.

The hypothesis being using this technique is this: In a linear regression, the upper limit of a response variable (i.e. NFL production) is theoretically limited by the measured predictor variable (i.e. NCAA production or Combine measurements). But, the response variable (NFL production) may change by less than expected when other limiting factors are present. Figure 1 below shows four different hypothetical example data sets illustrating how limiting factors can control responses. Figure 1.A shows a direct linear relationship, where only the measured predictor, NCAA Sacks per Game, limits how many NFL sacks per game a player has. Figure 1.B shows what the data looks like when an additional limiting factor is present, but not measured. This additional factor could be a player's body weight or height. Figure 1.C shows more than one limiting factor for a number of players (represented by the data points). In Figure 1.D, we see many unmeasured limiting factors for many of the players, resulting in a wedge-shaped distribution.

1.A Measured predictor variable (NCAA sacks) is only limiting factor.

1.B There is one other factor besides NCAA sacks that is limiting "NFL sacks per Game."

1.C Some unmeasured limiting factors some players' "NFL sacks per Game."

1.D Many unmeasured limiting factors limiting players' "NFL sacks per Game."

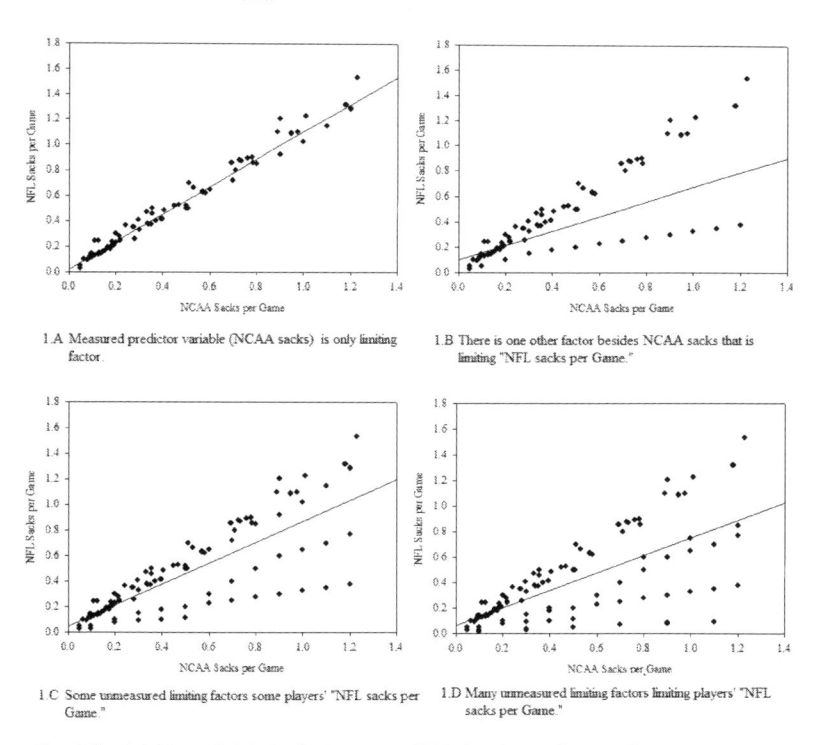

Figure 1: Hypothetical data set displaying the effect that un-measured limiting factors have on a linear regression.

So, using Quantile Regression, I explored what Combine metrics appear to "limit" NFL potential. I will discuss these findings position-by-position.

The Offensive Line

Everything starts up front right? I begin my analysis of the NFL Combine with the offensive line. I analyzed the 50th, 75th, and 95th quantiles of relationships between the 40 yard dash, the 20 yard shuttle, the 3-cone drill, and the vertical leap and each players' Career Approximate Value for 121 offensive tackles, 90 offensive guards, and 42 centers. Traditionally a regression line splits the data with 50% below the line and 50% above. In my quantile regression I also include the 75th and 95th quantiles, meaning that those lines split the data 75% / 25% and 95% / 5% respectively. This allowed me to quantify the strength of the correlations of the highest responders in the population. An example of a 95th percentile responder would be JJ Watt, while a 50th percentile responder would be Mario Williams. Both players had similarly impressive combine performances, with Williams performing slightly better. But, Watt appears to reach a higher level of NFL production, or he reaches the fullest potential of that raw athletic talent, while Williams' NFL production is about average for his athleticism.

In this study on offensive lineman, I found that the ability to predict potential was best for the offensive guards. The 40 yard dash was most highly correlated with successful NFL guards. The vertical leap correlated well with both centers and tackles. The short shuttle correlated with centers. And the 3-cone drill also correlated with guards. The figures below display correlations between 40 yard dash, the short shuttle run, the 3-cone drill, and the vertical leap, and offensive line CarAV in the NFL.

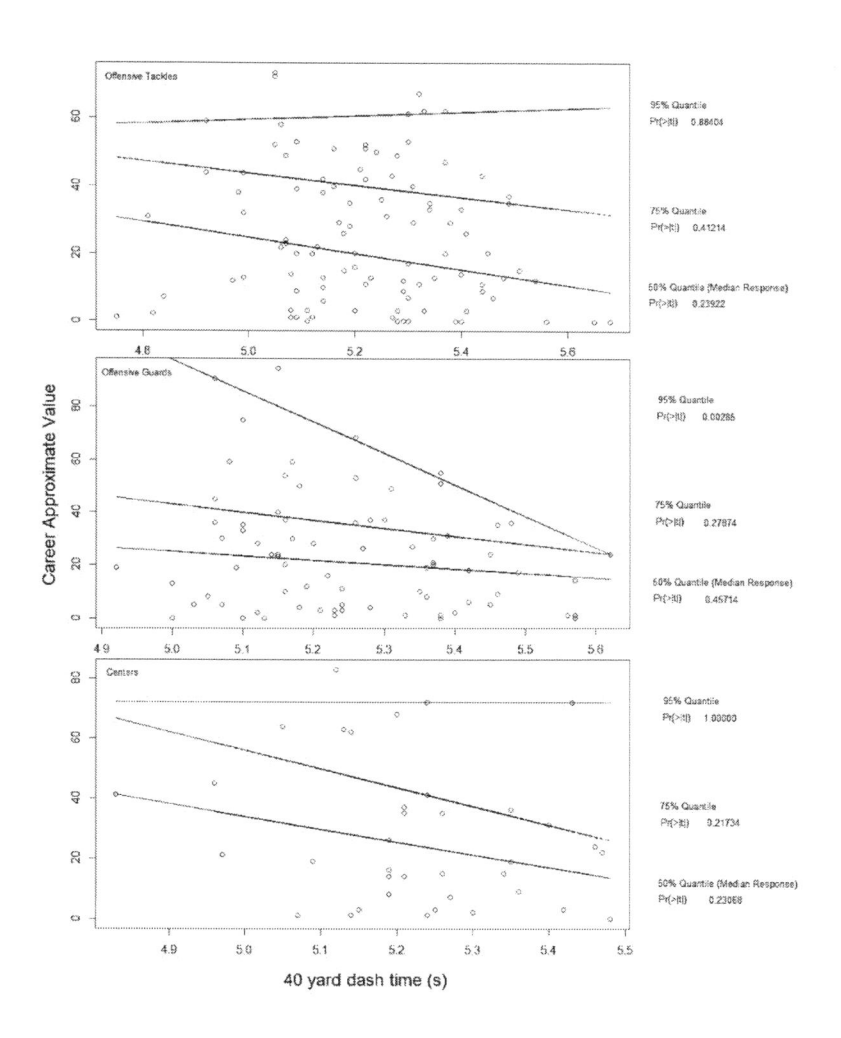

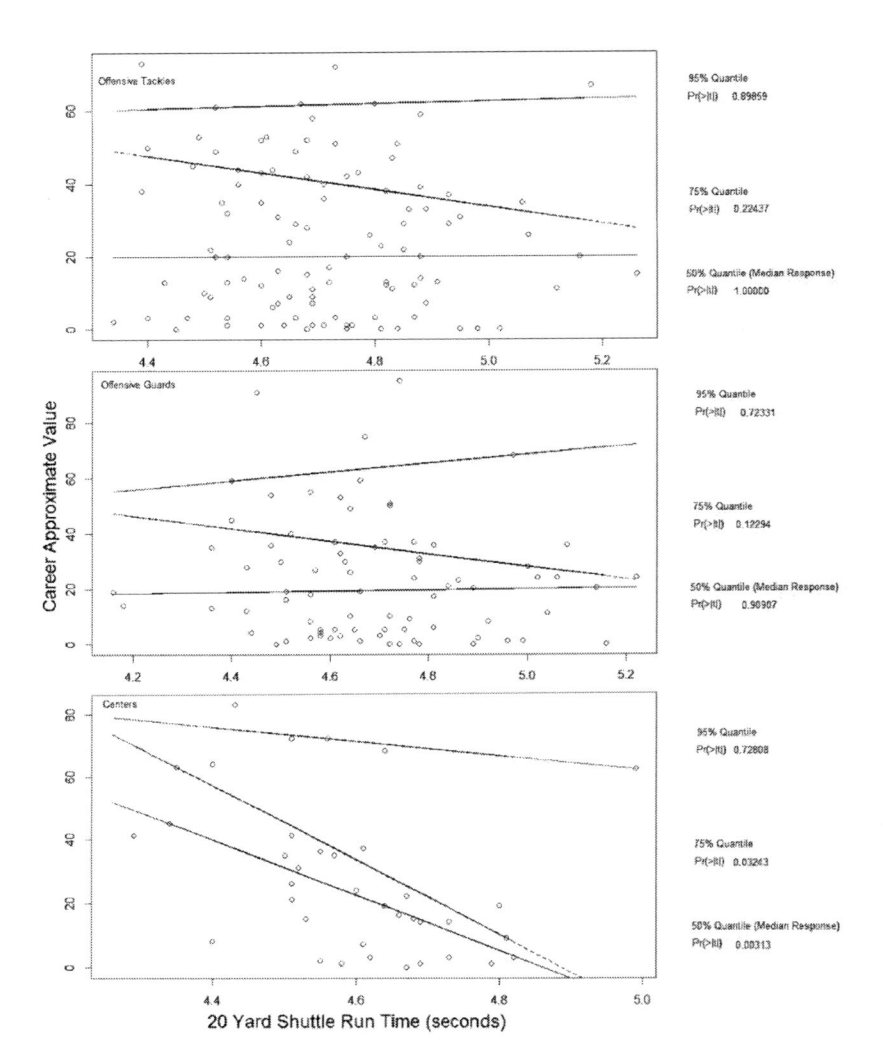

Offensive Tackles	95% Quantile	Pr(>|t|) 0.89859
	75% Quantile	Pr(>|t|) 0.22437
	50% Quantile (Median Response)	Pr(>|t|) 1.00000
Offensive Guards	95% Quantile	Pr(>|t|) 0.72331
	75% Quantile	Pr(>|t|) 0.12294
	50% Quantile (Median Response)	Pr(>|t|) 0.90907
Centers	95% Quantile	Pr(>|t|) 0.72808
	75% Quantile	Pr(>|t|) 0.03243
	50% Quantile (Median Response)	Pr(>|t|) 0.00313

Career Approximate Value vs. 20 Yard Shuttle Run Time (seconds)

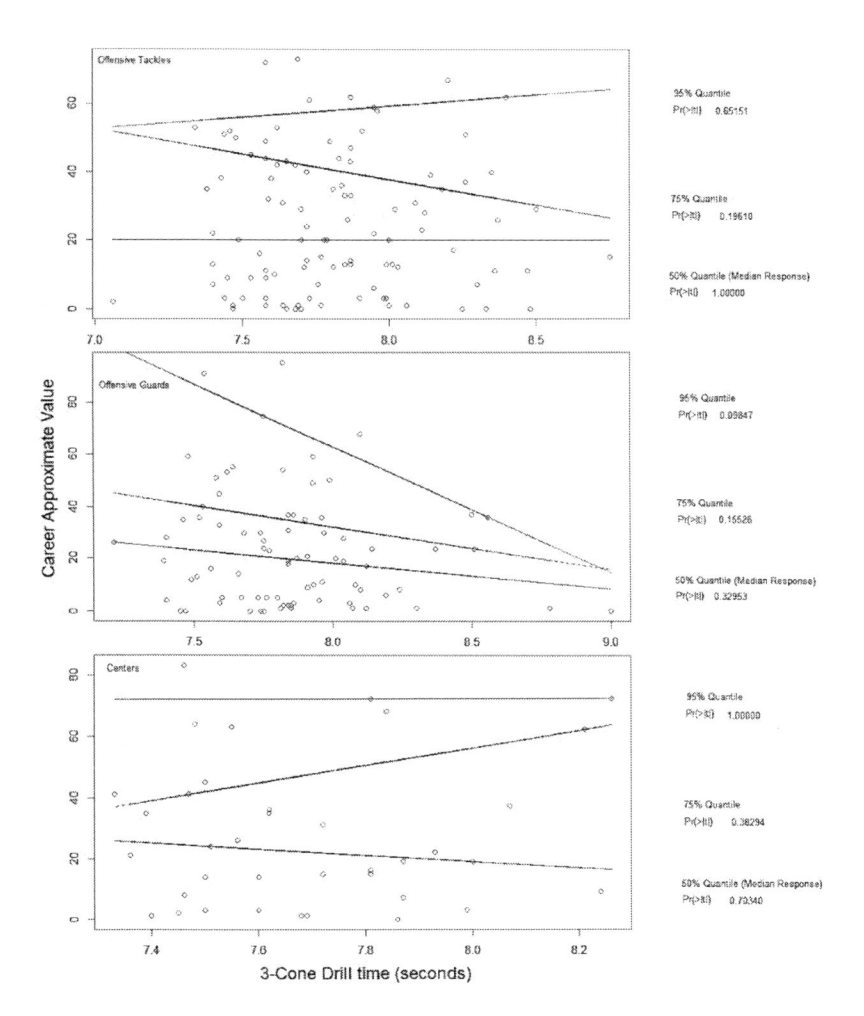

	Offensive Tackles	95% Quantile
		Pr(>|t|) 0.65151
		75% Quantile
		Pr(>|t|) 0.19610
		50% Quantile (Median Response)
		Pr(>|t|) 1.00000

	Offensive Guards	95% Quantile
		Pr(>|t|) 0.06847
		75% Quantile
		Pr(>|t|) 0.15526
		50% Quantile (Median Response)
		Pr(>|t|) 0.32953

	Centers	95% Quantile
		Pr(>|t|) 1.00000
		75% Quantile
		Pr(>|t|) 0.38294
		50% Quantile (Median Response)
		Pr(>|t|) 0.70340

Career Approximate Value vs. 3-Cone Drill time (seconds)

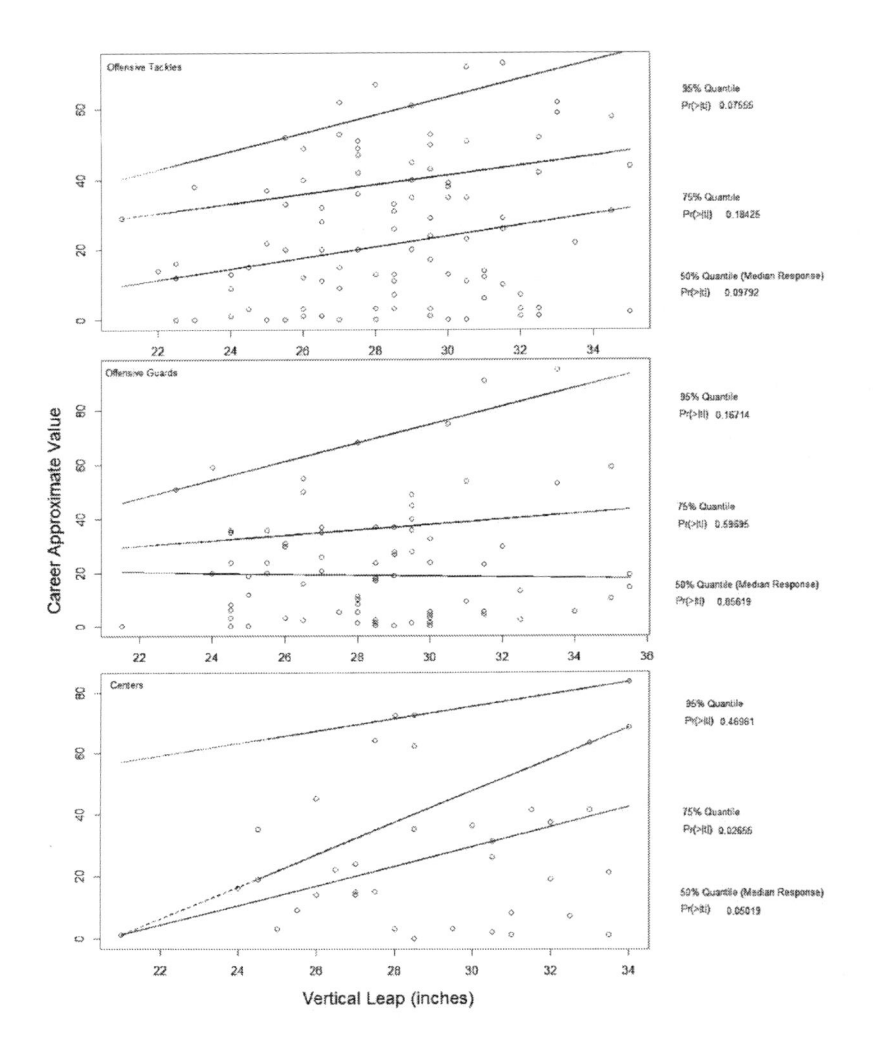

Running Backs, Wide Receivers, and Tight Ends

Skill position players rely on speed, agility, and elusiveness, and often are the most exciting performers at the NFL Combine. Chris Johnson ran the fastest modern 40 yard dash time in modern Combine history, at 4.24 seconds. Calvin Johnson borrowed shoes to run a 4.35 at 239 pounds. Vernon Davis re-established what the tight end position was capable of with a 4.38 40 yard dash, and a 42 inch vertical leap while weighing 254 pounds. Chris Johnson, Calvin Johnson, and Vernon Davis have all gone on to produce historically great numbers in the NFL. But… are speed and leaping measurements indicative of NFL success for these skill positions so reliant on elite athleticism?

Only NFL production for the maximum potential quantile (95th quantile) of running backs was significantly correlated with their 40 yard dash time at the NFL combine. Tight end potential at the 75th quantile was significantly correlated to 40 yard dash times. There did appear to be a bi-modal distribution of Tight End 40 yard dash time vs Career Approximate Value. This is presumably because a tight ends' role in the NFL is either as a blocker or receiver, and there are different physical skill sets required for each.

Interestingly, NFL Career Approximate Value (CarAV) of wide receivers was not significantly correlated with two measurements typically understood to be very important to their success: 40 yard dash time and vertical leap. Tight end, rather, was the only position that seemed to correlate with vertical leap. Neither the 3-cone drill, nor the shuttle run were significant predictors for any of the three skill positions. Initially, I was surprised to discover a lack of correlation between the agility tests and skill position success in the NFL. However, most times recorded at the

Combine are already elite, and elite agility is probably a prerequisite to play at a high level in college. This suggests that there are other factors dictating what makes athletes successful beyond college, and in the NFL. Deceptiveness, suddenness, and reaction times seem quite important for these skill positions, but those attributes are much harder to quantify.

Running Backs

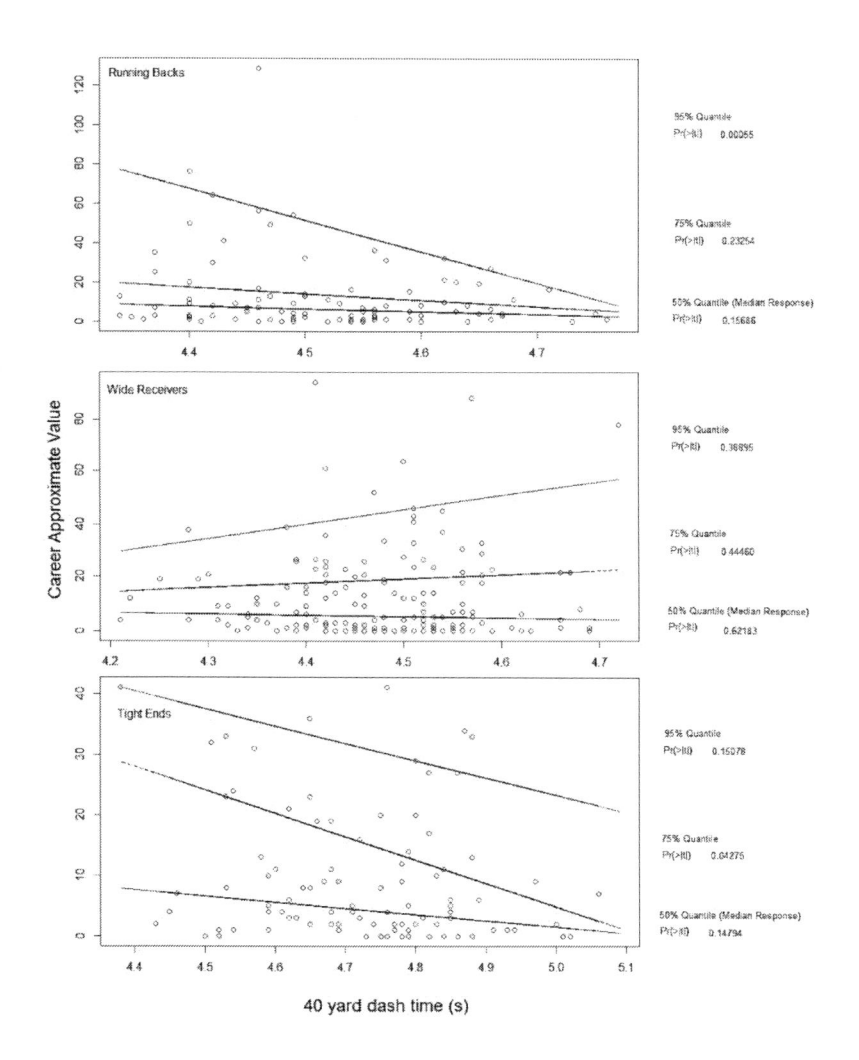

95% Quantile	
Pr(>|t|)	0.00055
75% Quantile	
Pr(>|t|)	0.23254
50% Quantile (Median Response)	
Pr(>|t|)	0.15686

Wide Receivers

95% Quantile	
Pr(>|t|)	0.36895
75% Quantile	
Pr(>|t|)	0.44460
50% Quantile (Median Response)	
Pr(>|t|)	0.62183

Tight Ends

95% Quantile	
Pr(>|t|)	0.15078
75% Quantile	
Pr(>|t|)	0.04275
50% Quantile (Median Response)	
Pr(>|t|)	0.14794

Career Approximate Value

40 yard dash time (s)

Running Backs

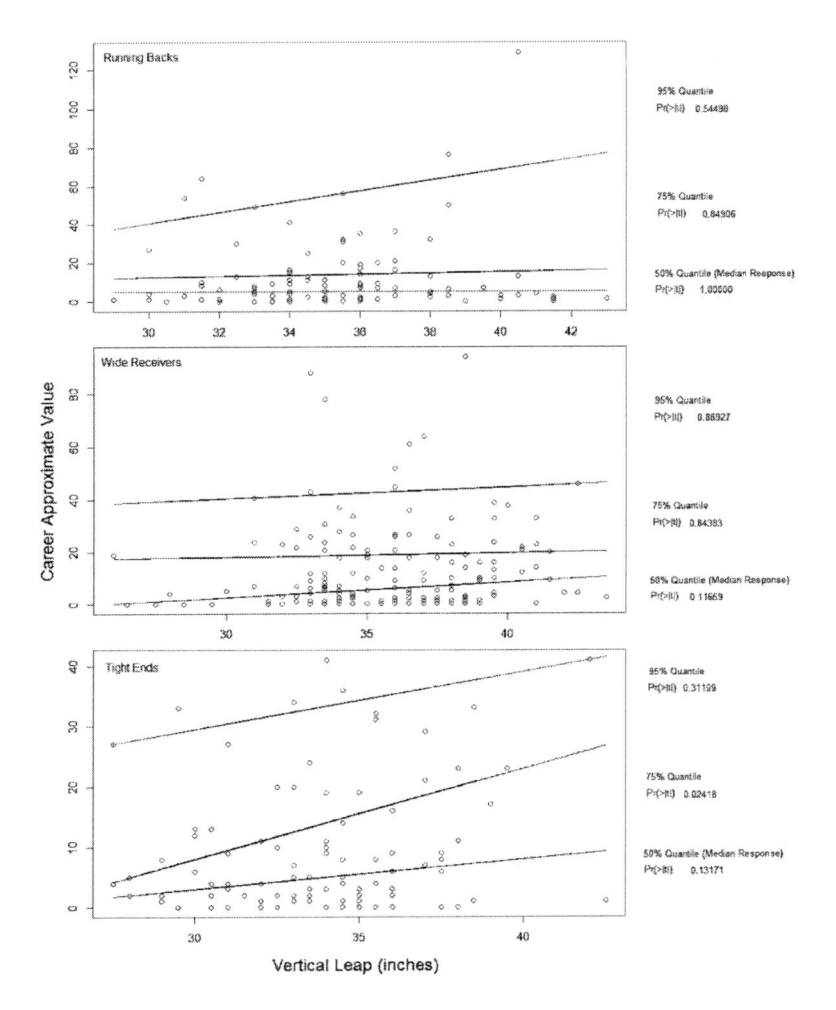

95% Quantile
Pr(>|t|) 0.54498

75% Quantile
Pr(>|t|) 0.84906

50% Quantile (Median Response)
Pr(>|t|) 1.00000

Wide Receivers

95% Quantile
Pr(>|t|) 0.86927

75% Quantile
Pr(>|t|) 0.84383

50% Quantile (Median Response)
Pr(>|t|) 0.11669

Tight Ends

95% Quantile
Pr(>|t|) 0.31199

75% Quantile
Pr(>|t|) 0.02418

50% Quantile (Median Response)
Pr(>|t|) 0.13171

Vertical Leap (inches)

Career Approximate Value

Running Backs

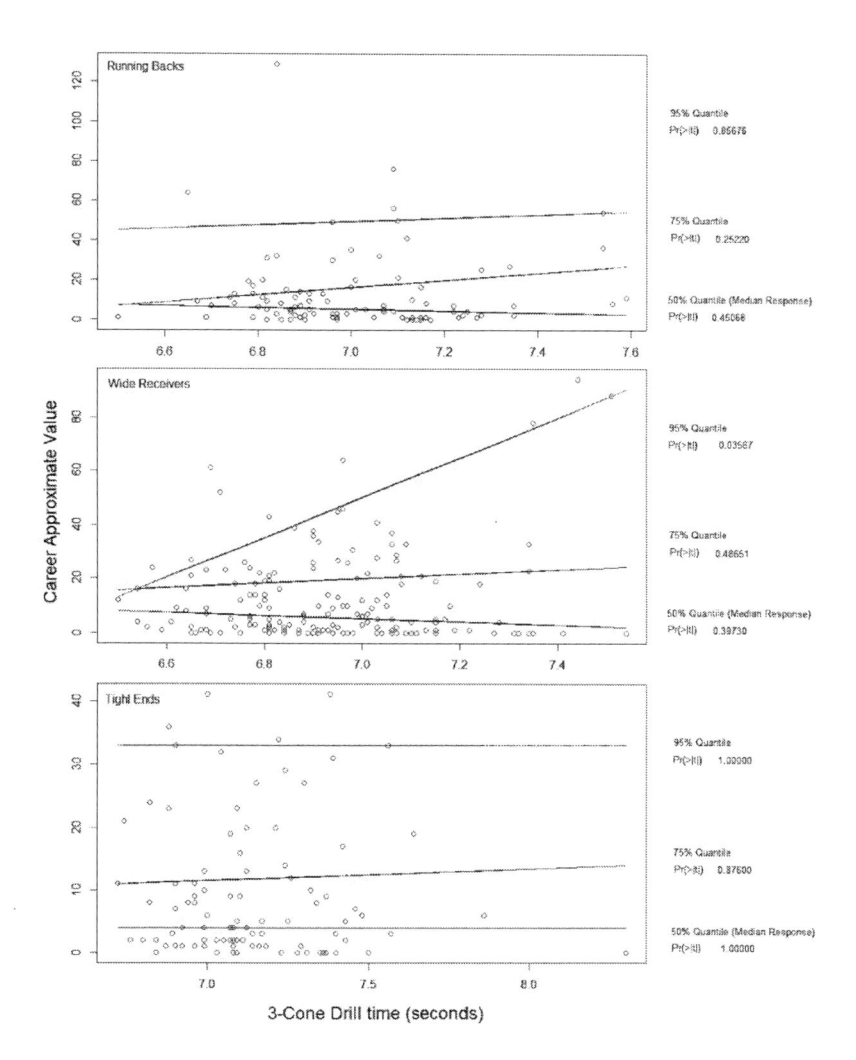

95% Quantile
Pr(>|t|) 0.85676

75% Quantile
Pr(>|t|) 0.25220

50% Quantile (Median Response)
Pr(>|t|) 0.45068

Wide Receivers

95% Quantile
Pr(>|t|) 0.03587

75% Quantile
Pr(>|t|) 0.48651

50% Quantile (Median Response)
Pr(>|t|) 0.39730

Tight Ends

95% Quantile
Pr(>|t|) 1.00000

75% Quantile
Pr(>|t|) 0.87600

50% Quantile (Median Response)
Pr(>|t|) 1.00000

Career Approximate Value

3-Cone Drill time (seconds)

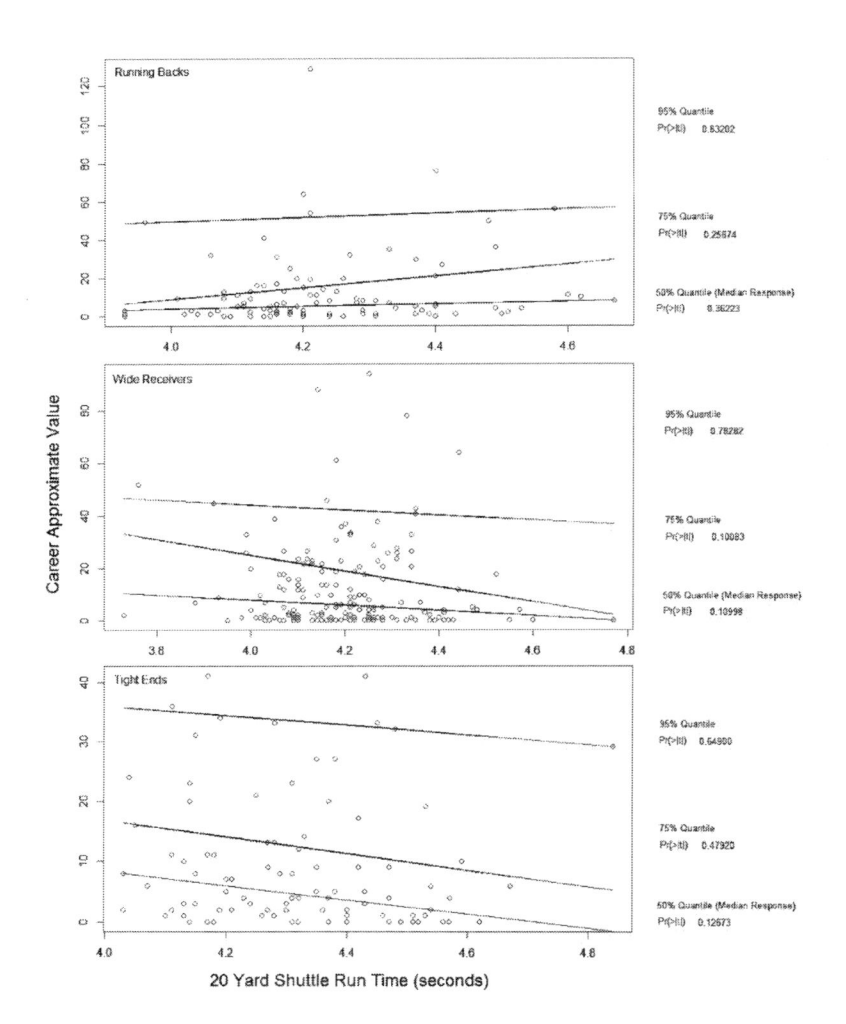

Defensive Line and Linebackers

Some scouts argue that the defensive linemen is the position most reliant on innate athleticism. A combination of size, speed, power, and an overall freaky combination of athleticism is vital for playing on the defensive side of the line. Although these players do need to utilize leverage, play with their hands, and anticipate, a prospect's size, speed, and lower body explosiveness are all very important to an evaluation. When thinking of the elite defensive lineman in the league, athletic freaks come to mind. At the NFL Combine, perennial All-Pro Geno Atkins ran a sub 4.8 second 40 yard dash, and broad jumped nearly 10 feet while weighing 293 pounds. Ndamukong Suh and Gerald McCoy both lit up the 2010 Combine, and have since performed at All-Pro levels. J.J. Watt and Mario Williams were perhaps the freakiest athletes ever to attend the Combine, jumping 37 and 40.5 inches respectively in the vertical, while both weighed over 290 pounds. While it is possible that these members of the 2013 NFL All-Pro team are simply outliers, there does appear to be an overarching correlative trend between Combine metrics and NFL production on the defensive line.

Linebackers are often referred to as the quarterbacks of the defense. While they must possess exceptional lateral quickness, anticipation, and recognition skills, they also need to be able to audible or shift alignment. Linebacker is a position that appears to require many more intangible, or unmeasured, skills than that of the defensive line. However, the NFL's best linebackers are also athletic freaks of nature: Patrick Willis (4.37 second 40 yard dash at his Ole Miss pro day) and Luke Kuechly (a top performer in nearly every combine drill that has been discussed already).

In terms of linear speed, defensive tackle and linebacker showed significant correlations between 40 yard dash time and Career Approximate Value (CarAV), for the 50th quantile. Likewise, defensive tackle and linebacker CarAV was also correlated to the vertical leap. The 3-cone drill, a movement drill thought to be representative of an edge rusher's ability to "turn-the-corner", was significantly correlated with both defensive end and linebacker CarAV in the NFL. One would think that a fast short shuttle run time would be crucial to success of a linebacker, but in this dataset, the short shuttle run time does not help in predicting which linebackers succeed in the NFL, and which do not.

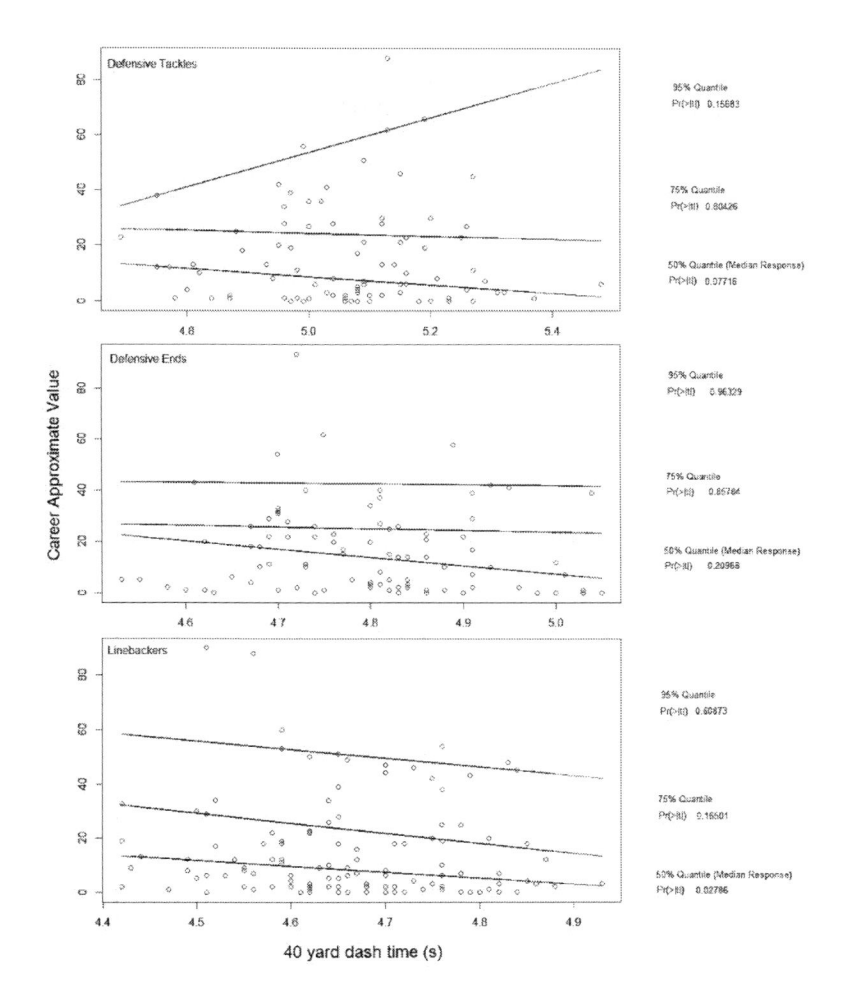

Defensive Tackles

95% Quantile
Pr(>|t|) 0.15883

75% Quantile
Pr(>|t|) 0.80426

50% Quantile (Median Response)
Pr(>|t|) 0.07716

Defensive Ends

95% Quantile
Pr(>|t|) 0.96329

75% Quantile
Pr(>|t|) 0.85764

50% Quantile (Median Response)
Pr(>|t|) 0.20968

Linebackers

95% Quantile
Pr(>|t|) 0.60873

75% Quantile
Pr(>|t|) 0.16601

50% Quantile (Median Response)
Pr(>|t|) 0.02786

Career Approximate Value

40 yard dash time (s)

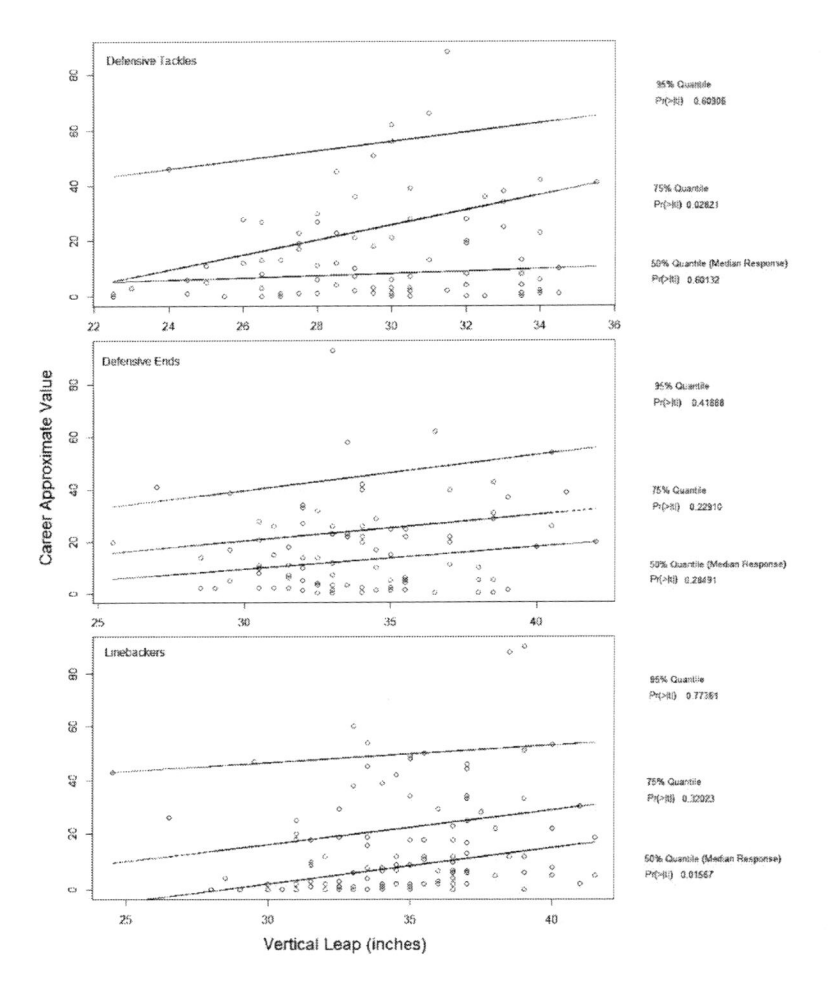

Defensive Tackles

95% Quantile
Pr(>|t|) 0.60306

75% Quantile
Pr(>|t|) 0.02821

50% Quantile (Median Response)
Pr(>|t|) 0.60132

Defensive Ends

95% Quantile
Pr(>|t|) 0.41888

75% Quantile
Pr(>|t|) 0.22910

50% Quantile (Median Response)
Pr(>|t|) 0.28491

Linebackers

95% Quantile
Pr(>|t|) 0.77361

75% Quantile
Pr(>|t|) 0.32023

50% Quantile (Median Response)
Pr(>|t|) 0.01567

Career Approximate Value

Vertical Leap (inches)

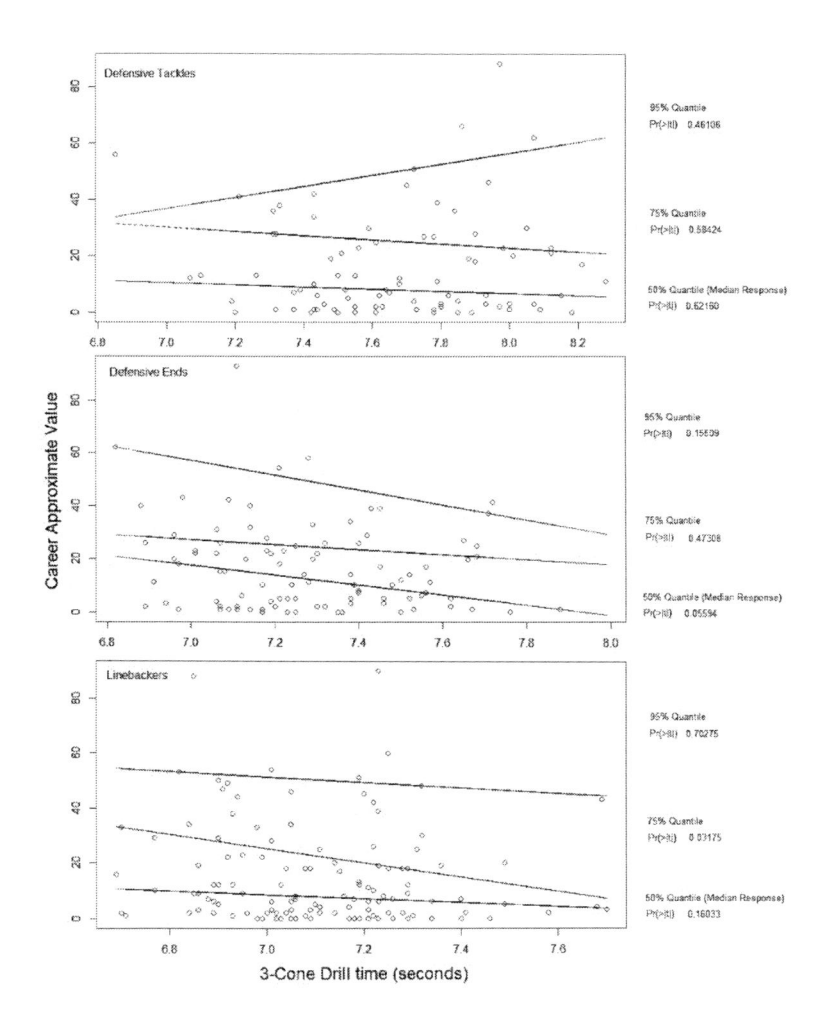

Defensive Tackles

95% Quantile
Pr(>|t|) 0.46106

75% Quantile
Pr(>|t|) 0.58424

50% Quantile (Median Response)
Pr(>|t|) 0.62160

Defensive Ends

95% Quantile
Pr(>|t|) 0.15509

75% Quantile
Pr(>|t|) 0.47308

50% Quantile (Median Response)
Pr(>|t|) 0.05594

Linebackers

95% Quantile
Pr(>|t|) 0.70275

75% Quantile
Pr(>|t|) 0.03175

50% Quantile (Median Response)
Pr(>|t|) 0.16033

Career Approximate Value

3-Cone Drill time (seconds)

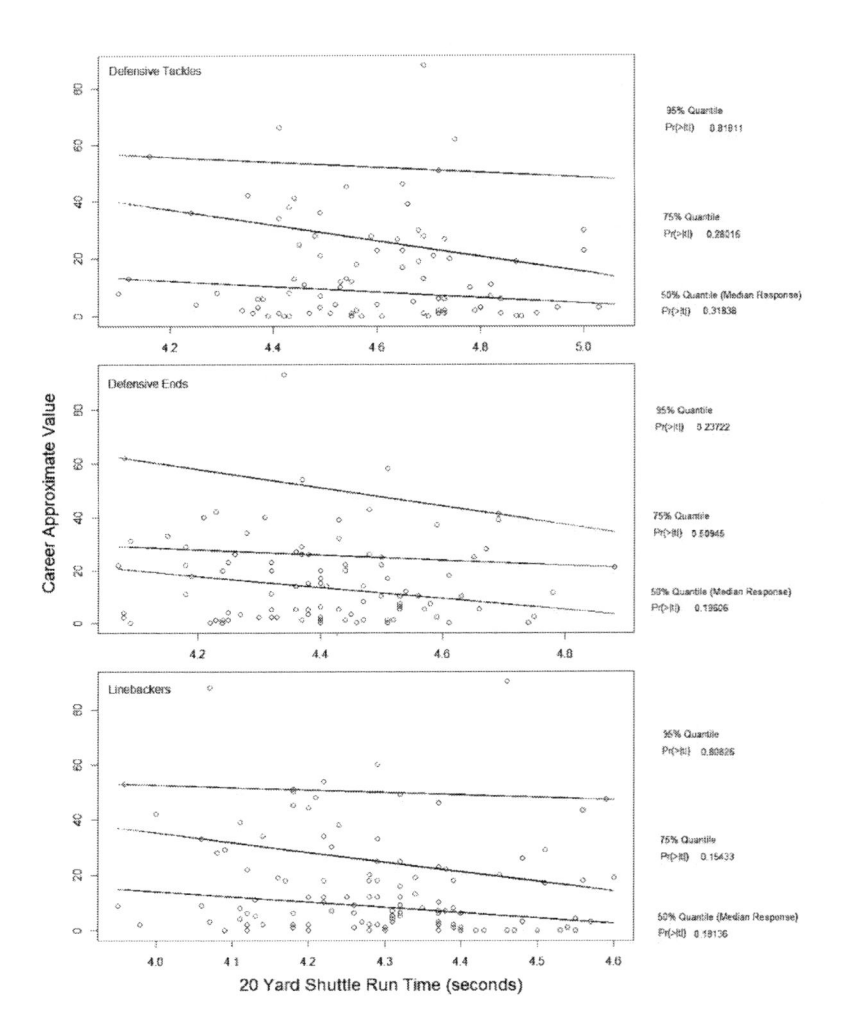

Defensive Backs

An NFL cornerback must match the athleticism of the League's top receivers…and also *react* to it. Therefore, successful cornerbacks must equal, or more likely, exceed the speed, quickness, and leaping ability of receivers. And that is essentially what I observed in this Quantile Regression study: the Career Approximate Value (CarAV) of cornerbacks in the NFL was significantly correlated with 40 yard dash time, vertical leap, and the shuttle run. The analysis of cornerbacks using Quantile Regression was the most clear and convincing evidence that data from the NFL Combine can be indicative of future NFL production.

Playing safety in the NFL appears to require many of the same skills needed to play both cornerback and linebacker. A safety must be able to read offenses and adjust coverage accordingly, instinctually break on passes or running plays, cover receivers one-on-one, and explosively tackle ball-carriers. The best safeties of the last decade have all had superb instincts, and elite athleticism: Troy Polamalu, Sean Taylor and Ed Reed. It appears that playing in space, like safeties do, relies much more on linear speed than short area quickness. What this Quantile Regression revealed was that 40 yard dash time was significantly indicative of a safety's ability to play in the NFL. Vertical leap was convincingly, but insignificantly correlated with Career AV, while the 3-cone and shuttle run had no discernable relationship.

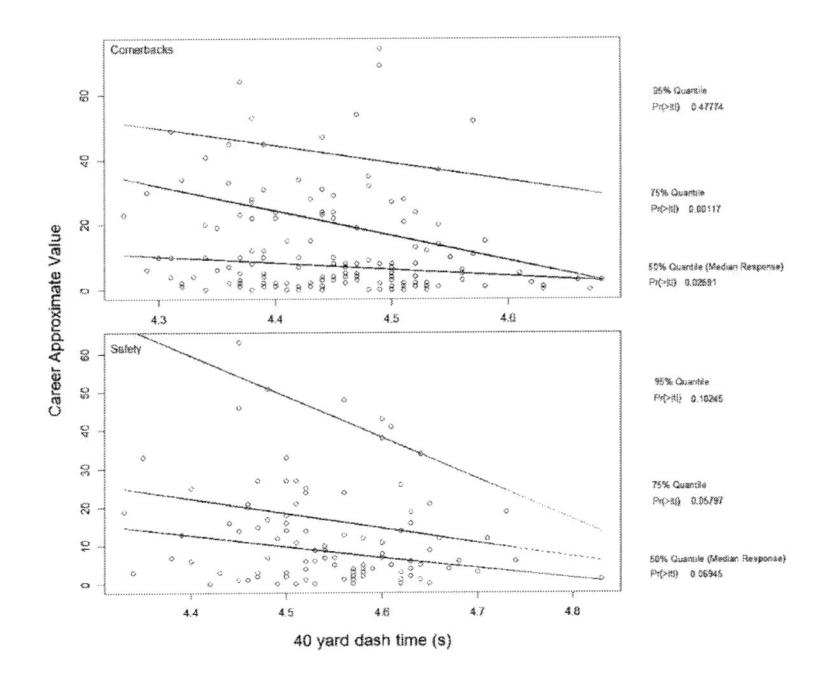

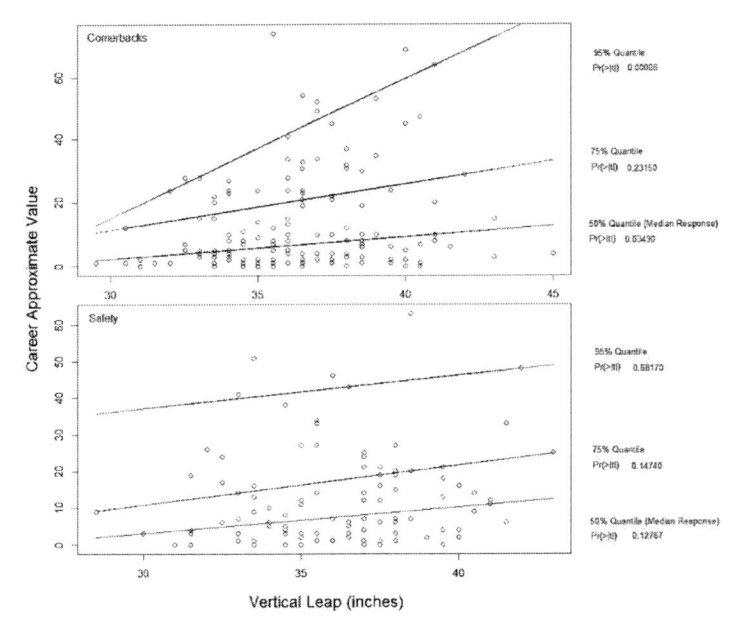

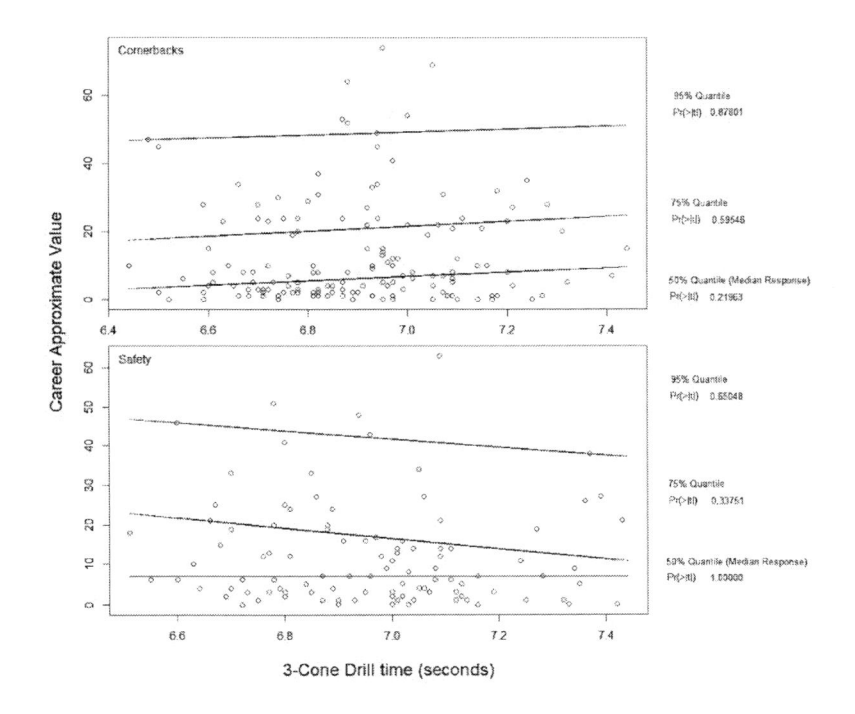

Cornerbacks

95% Quantile
Pr(>|t|) 0.87801

75% Quantile
Pr(>|t|) 0.59548

50% Quantile (Median Response)
Pr(>|t|) 0.21963

Safety

95% Quantile
Pr(>|t|) 0.65048

75% Quantile
Pr(>|t|) 0.33751

50% Quantile (Median Response)
Pr(>|t|) 1.00000

Career Approximate Value

3-Cone Drill time (seconds)

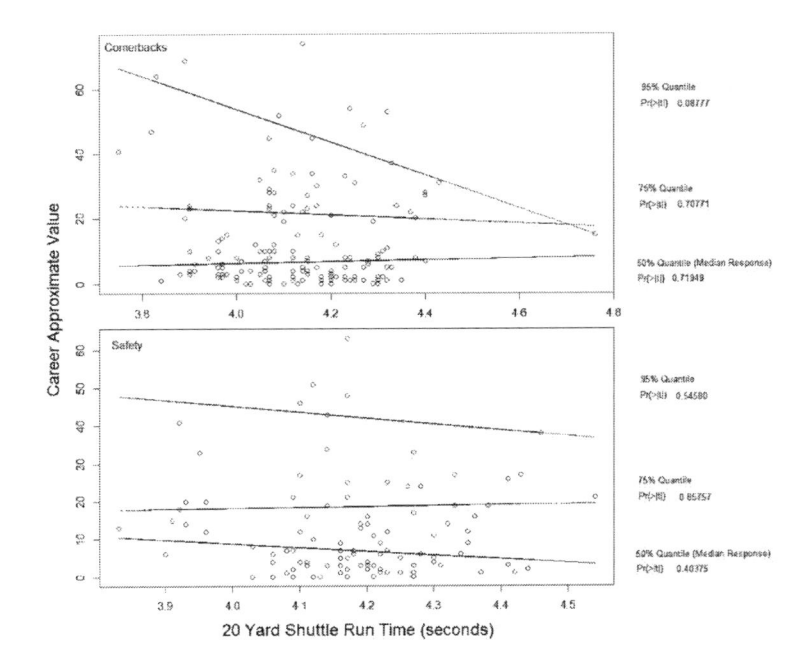

In Conclusion

Does the NFL Combine matter? So often, people want to pick a side in this debate, but the answer actually is: *Sometimes*. Football is an immensely complex team game, with an extreme amount of positional specialization. So naturally, different positions require different physical tool sets. Some positions like offensive guard, running back, or cornerback are clearly reliant on skills specifically measured (or at least measured by a reliable surrogate) at the NFL combine: linear speed, lateral quickness, and lower body explosiveness. Other positions like quarterback, linebacker, and center are not as easily predicted based on these drills. I believe interpretation of Combine data could be improved through a better understanding of what type of human physiology is necessary for a given position. Academic research shows that 40 yard dash and vertical leap are metrics of a human's posterior-chain power, and lower-body explosiveness. Through this Quantile Regression analysis of the NFL Combine, I try to show that particular athletic attributes are indeed requisite for playing *some* positions in the NFL. Clearly, not every position in the NFL requires an elite ability to change direction, or a fast 40 yard dash. Before interpreting data, talent evaluators must first ask: What does the position require? How can we measure that? Where does this player rank in terms of the historical successful NFL population? Therein lies the greatest utility of data collected from the NFL Combine.

Power Output and Pass Rushing

In an athletic context, power can be understood as the combination of forces and movement. Specifically, power is the product of a force on an object and the object's velocity. In the example of an athlete, power is the product of force produced by an athlete that translates to the propulsion of that athlete and thus their velocity. The vertical leap is not only one of the core metrics at the NFL Combine, but it is also one of the most popular and easy ways to assess power output of an athlete. As technology improves, there will be more accurate and elegant ways to measure power output. However, currently, these methods of measurement require force platforms, force plate treadmills, time-of-flight measures, and even film analysis. A simple mechanical power formula was devised for both peak and average power using a typical vertical leap (aka countermovement jump and reach test) by Johnson and Bahamonde (1996). This formula incorporates an athlete's height, weight, and vertical leap to estimate both peak and average power output.

I've been interested in power output of NFL prospects for many years. Data demonstrates that speed or leaping ability in the NFL almost never matters in the absence of body mass. In other words, NFL athletes must have a combination of body mass, speed, agility, explosiveness, etc. in order to be successful. The best players in the NFL are not simultaneously the fastest or highest jumpers in the world. A review of over 3000 NFL Combine invitees revealed a strong correlation between weight and speed; speed was inversely related to body weight.

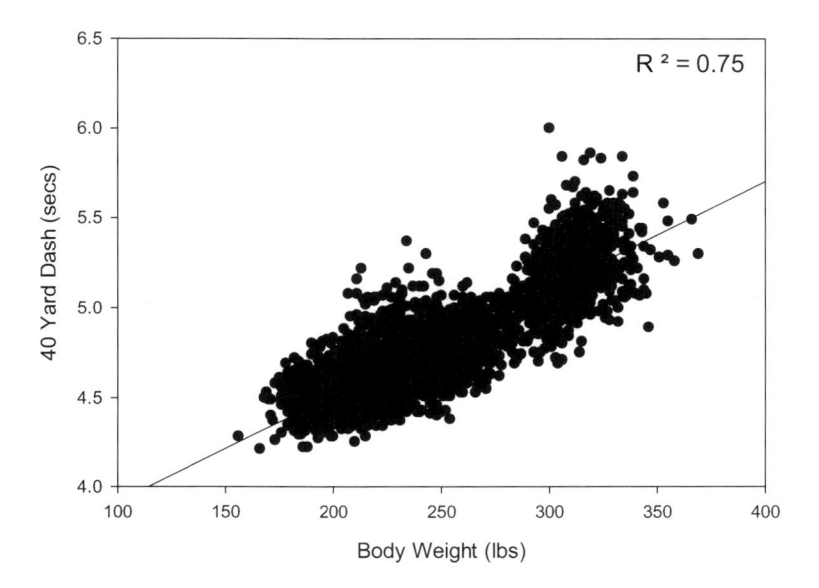

Based on that data, body weight was able to explain roughly 75% of the variance observed in 40 yard dash times. Using the formula from that relationship (shown below), I predicted 40 yard dash times for each prospect.

$$40 \text{ yard dash time (secs)} = 0.0059 \times Body\ Weight\ (lbs) + 3.34$$

The difference between the predicted 40 yard dash time (aka: what each player is predicted to run based on the equation above, and their own bodyweight), and what they did run, can be used to identify the fastest "pound-for-pound" athlete to ever attend the combine. Running 0.46

seconds faster than his predicted time, Vernon Davis is the fastest "pound-for-pound" combine invitee of all time. The Table below lists the Top 20 All-Time.

Year	Name	College	POS	Height (in)	Weight (lbs)	40 Yard Dash (secs)	Predicted 40 Yard Dash (secs)	(+/-) 40
2006	Vernon Davis	Maryland	TE	75	254	4.38	4.84	-0.46
2004	Tank Johnson	Washington	DT	75	304	4.69	5.14	-0.45
2010	Bruce Campbell	Maryland	OT	79	314	4.75	5.20	-0.45
2013	Terron Armstead	Arkansas-Pine Bluff	OT	77	306	4.71	5.15	-0.44
2013	Lane Johnson	Oklahoma	OT	78	303	4.72	5.13	-0.41
2011	Dontay Moch	Nevada	OLB	73	248	4.4	4.81	-0.41
2012	Dontari Poe	Memphis	DT	76	346	4.98	5.39	-0.41
2012	James Hanna	Oklahoma	TE	76	252	4.43	4.83	-0.40
2011	Martez Wilson	Illinois	ILB	76	250	4.42	4.82	-0.40
2012	Nick Perry	Southern California	DE	75	271	4.55	4.94	-0.39
2010	Trent Williams	Oklahoma	OT	77	315	4.81	5.20	-0.39
2006	Mario Williams	North Carolina State	DE	79	295	4.7	5.09	-0.39
2009	Lawrence Sidbury	Richmond	DE	75	266	4.53	4.91	-0.38
2014	Greg Robinson	Auburn	OT	77	332	4.92	5.30	-0.38
2012	Bruce Irvin	West Virginia	OLB	75	245	4.41	4.79	-0.38
2011	Von Miller	Texas A&M	OLB	75	246	4.42	4.80	-0.38
2015	Alvin Dupree	Kentucky	DE	76	269	4.56	4.93	-0.37
2005	Brandon Jacobs	Southern Illinois	RB	76	267	4.56	4.92	-0.36
2013	Margus Hunt	Southern Methodist	DE	80	277	4.62	4.98	-0.36
2016	Charles Tapper	Oklahoma	DE	74.63	271	4.59	4.94	-0.35

What stands out about this list is the number of standout pass rushers and pass protectors. Dontari Poe, Mario Williams, and Von Miller are All-Pro defensive players, while Lane Johnson, Trent Williams, and Terron Armstead have also made All-Pro and Pro-Bowl teams. This data suggested that weight-adjusted speed/explosiveness or even more simply, a combination of body mass and athletic ability, was important for playing football around the line of scrimmage. And that combination of mass and that ability to accelerate that mass can very basically be translated into power or force production.

My next question was "How do I estimate force and power?" Force would be very difficult to estimate without time interval measurements for the 40 yard dash. The next best option was using the vertical or broad jump measurements to estimate power. However, as mentioned earlier, power cannot be calculated (*power = work / time*) without a measurement of time, or without technology such as directly measuring using a force plate. But, within scientific literature formula have been derived that estimate power from vertical jump measurements. So using one of these formula derived by Johnson and Bahamonde (1996), I estimated peak and average power for each NFL Combine attendee from 2000 to 2017. However, this would only tell me how much power was generated in the vertical direction. And literature suggests that in order to maximize horizontal acceleration (which is typically what is most important in football), athletes should produce only enough vertical force to raise their center of mass so that they can recycle their limbs and reapply horizontal force during acceleration. And, only once maximum speed is reached, is vertical force production correlated with sprinting performance. Therefore, I went ahead and predicted power using Johnson and Bahamonde's formula with both vertical and broad jump heights.

Year	Name	College	POS	Weight (lbs)	Vertical Leap (in)	Johnson & Bahamonde Avg Power (W)	Johnson & Bahamonde Peak Power (W)
2009	Chris Baker	Hampton	DT	326	35.5	6068	11839
2006	Mario Williams	North Carolina State	DE	295	40.5	5950	11793
2009	Travis Bright	BYU	OG	321	35.5	5909	11624
2011	Marcus Cannon	Texas Christian	OT	358	30.5	5860	11601
2010	Al Woods	Louisiana State	DT	309	37	5897	11595

Year	Name	College	POS	Weight (lbs)	Vertical Leap (in)	Johnson & Bahamonde Avg Power (W)	Johnson & Bahamonde Peak Power (W)
2015	Byron Jones	Connecticut	CB	199	147	16643	30671
2015	Alvin "Bud" Dupree	Kentucky	DE	269	138	16539	30662
2013	Jamie Collins	Southern Mississippi	OLB	250	139	16367	30341
2017	Obi Melifonwu	Connecticut	FS	224	141	16203	30027
2017	Bucky Hodges	Virginia Tech	TE	257	134	15824	29452

Looking through the list of players with the highest estimates for power output, any significance appears to be fairly position-specific. For instance, the Top 5 Defensive Ends ever in terms of estimated vertical power output are a pretty compelling case:

Year	Name	College	POS	Weight (lbs)	Vertical Leap (in)	Johnson & Bahamonde Avg Power (W)	Johnson & Bahamonde Peak Power (W)
2006	Mario Williams	North Carolina State	DE	295	40.5	5950	11793
2015	Alvin "Bud" Dupree	Kentucky	DE	269	42	5859	11497
2017	Myles Garrett	Texas A&M	DE	272	41	5782	11369
2006	Mark Anderson	Alabama	DE	254	42	5636	11085
2011	J.J. Watt	Wisconsin	DE	290	37	5572	11035

Similarly the Top 15 linebacker prospects ever according to estimated vertical power output include: Cameron Wake, Jamie Collins, Connor Barwin, Ryan Shazier, Vic Beasley, Khalil Mack, A.J. Hawk, and Justin Houston. Other positions are not nearly as compelling as the linebackers or pass rushers. While these estimations of power are only an isolated metric for a given athlete, I think that integrating approaches from other scientific disciplines holds much promise for interpreting data from the tests of athletic performance.

How Ecology Can Further NFL Analytics

As different as ecology and the NFL sound, they share quite similar problems. The environment is an infinitely complex system with many known and unknown variables. Researchers in the fields of ecology and environmental science often have to utilize multivariate statistical methods in order to answer questions about the environment. For instance, scientists often must determine whether a chemical/toxin is a risk to our environmental or public health. And environmental chemical exposures occur in infinitely complex mixtures with other chemicals, and they occur across many different environments. And, distinguishing any type of definitive trend from such dynamic situations is difficult. In the environmental and ecological sciences, scientists will sometimes use non-traditional methods to help visualize *noisy* data. From purely a data perspective, talent projections in sports exhibits a similar challenge in that NFL prospects are always a unique combination of their college team, inherent athleticism, history, intangibles, and even the current landscape in the NFL. The myriad of variables present in both environment and NFL datasets, both static and changing, make it difficult to separate the statistical "*noise*" from actual, observable trends.

> Note: Statistical *noise* is just a simple a term for recognized amounts of unexplained variability in a given dataset.

The NFL is a perpetually changing landscape with a revolving door of players and schemes. And predicting an athlete's performance pre-draft is complicated through a number of contributing variables including combine results, college production, unmeasured intangibles, and/or how well that player fits a certain NFL scheme. While working on this book, I thought perhaps techniques that ecologists use to discern confounding trends in nature may be suitable for such challenges as the NFL talent evaluations. This Chapter aims to introduce an eco-statistical tool, Principal Component Analysis (PCA), and describe its potential utility for interpreting NFL Draft-related datasets, and assessing NFL draft prospects.

Note: The following paragraph will discuss the *nuts and bolts* of Principal Component Analysis.

The purpose of Principal Component Analysis (PCA) is to represent a multivariate dataset (or a dataset containing many different variables) with a much smaller number of composite variables, or principal components. To conceptualize this idea, think of the QB Rating (QBR). The QBR is essentially a composite variable because it incorporates a number of other variables (Completion %, Yards, TDs, etc) into one number. PCA differs from a metric like the QBR in that a PCA places no bias on which variables it incorporates into the principal component. PCA only *chooses* the most compelling co-variation among variables, or the variables which explain the most variance between the sample units (i.e. Players). For this reasons, PCA can be useful in dissecting out what specific variables separate players in the NFL or college. By performing a PCA, I can visualize how similar each player or prospect is to each other. When I do this in a historical sense, I may be able to observe similarities between Pro Bowlers…or draft busts. By deconstructing the PCA, I can identify what Combine measurements (or stats, attributes, etc) are highly correlated to the principal components (composite variable). For instance, maybe 40 yard dash time or the vertical leap is highly correlated to a principal component, and bench press is not. The principal component (PC) itself can then be used as a predictor, or can be used to inform what variables are statistically most interesting.

I collected combine data from http://nflcombineresults.com/ , and I collected college and professional on-field statistics for each prospect from http://www.sports-reference.com/ . The NFL data will represent our dependent variables (Y axis), or what we hope to eventually predict. The NCAA statistics and NFL Combine measurements will be the independent variables, and what we use to predict NFL production. I was able to gather enough quality data for 82 defensive ends.

I then experimented by plotting different variables against each other. For example, I plotted bench press reps and 40 yard dash times versus career NFL sacks per game, for all 82 defensive ends (Figures 1 and 2). You can see that 40 yard dash time has a slight inverse relationship to career sacks per game (Figure 2), whereas bench press has virtually no correlation (Figure 1). This is not very surprising to most people knowledgeable about football. Further, the 40 yard dash data is wedge shaped (Figure 3). As 40 yard dash times get faster, the upper limit of career sacks per game increases. By looking at Figure 3, you can see that virtually no player running a 4.8 or slower (in the 40 yard dash) averages over a half sack per game. This suggests that 40 yard dash speed may "*cap*", or limit, the maximum potential, or "*ceiling*", of a pass rushing prospect. However, there are clearly other variables present that may also limit or dictate whether that potential is ever realized.

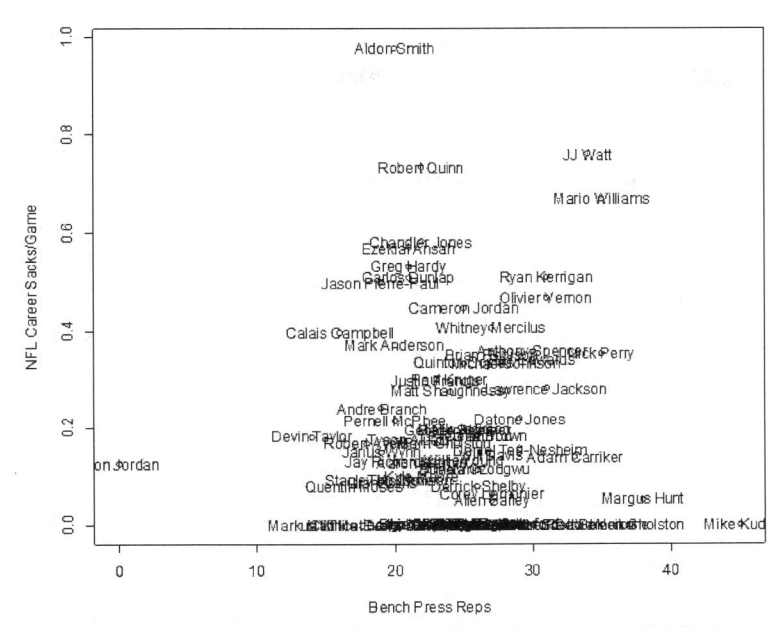

Figure 1: Combine bench press reps vs career NFL sacks per game for 82 defensive ends drafted over the past decade.

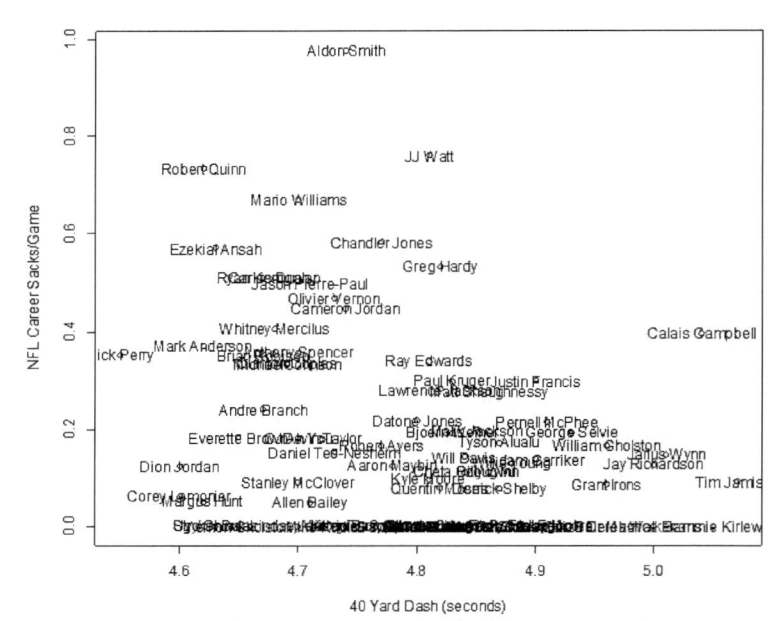

Figure 2: Combine 40 yard dash time vs Career NFL sacks per game for the group of 82 defensive ends.

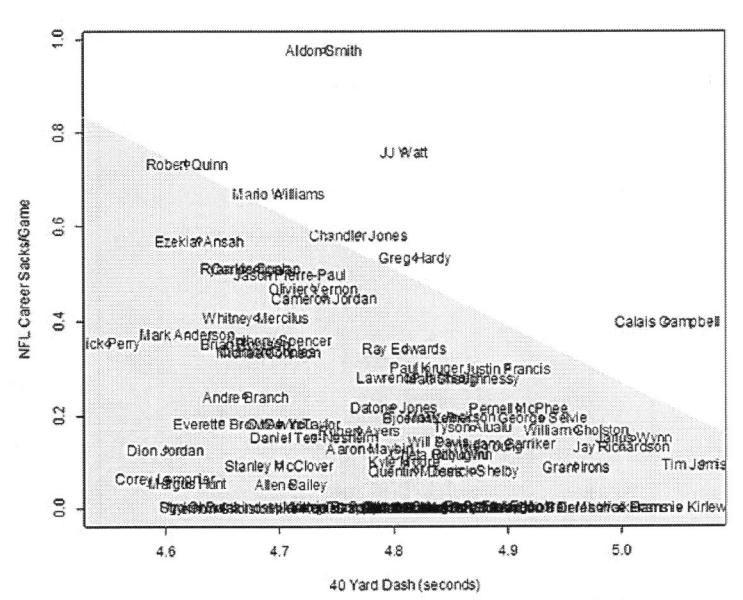

Figure 3: Same as figure 2, plotting 40 yard dash times vs career NFL sacks per game. Notice the wedge shaped nature of the data shaded in grey.

As the Figures 1-3 demonstrate, using only one variable at a time to predict a prospect's NFL success does not exactly work well. This is where ordination techniques, namely PCA, can be beneficial. Principal Components will explain what individual measurements explain the most variability between different prospects. And a PCA opens dialogue for logical explanations for any correlative observations. For instance, maybe a player's tackles for loss in college separate out players with "high motors" from those without. Weight-normalized vertical leap may explain how much innate explosive power a prospect has. By running a PCA, we can find out objectively what explains differences between players, rather than placing pre-emptive bias on measurements that we have been conditioned to value (40 yard dash, height, sacks, etc.). The PCA that I will run will incorporate the following (listed below) NCAA statistics and NFL Combine measurements (for 82 different defensive end prospects) into synthetic principal components.

NCAA Statistics	Combine Numbers
Games played	Height (in)
Solo tackles	Weight (lbs)
Assisted tackles	40 Yard (raw and normalized to bodyweight)
Total tackles	Bench Press (raw and normalized to bodyweight)
Tackles for loss	Vert Leap (in) (raw and normalized to bodyweight)
Sacks	Broad Jump (in) (raw and normalized to bodyweight)
Interceptions	Shuttle (raw and normalized to bodyweight)
Interceptions return yards	3Cone (raw and normalized to bodyweight)
Interception return TDs	
Pass defended	
Fumble recoveries	
Fumble return yards	
Fumble return TDs	
Forced fumbles	

Recall that a Principal Component (PC) is a synthetic variable, much like the QBR. A PC differs from QBR in that it looks for what variables explain the most variance between players, while the QBR preemptively determines what metrics (i.e. TDs, INTs, and Completion %) are most important. So Principal Component 1 (PC1), shown below, is the composite of the variables that are statistically most important. Each original NCAA statistic or Combine measurement has a specific *loading*, or correlation with the Principal Component (PC), which essentially weights its importance. Here is what the loadings look like for Principal Component 1 (PC1):

Metric	Correlation to PC1
Broad Jump (Normalized to Body Weight)	0.28443847
Vertical Leap (Normalized to Body Weight)	0.28372795
40 time (Normalized to Body Weight)	0.27767565
Shuttle (Normalized to Body Weight)	0.2759471
3 Cone Drill (Normalized to Body Weight)	0.26241971
Weight	0.23945002
Vertical Leap	0.19334879
Broad Jump	0.1419384
Height	0.11334387
Bench Press Reps	0.11257059
Bench Press (Normalized to Body Weight)	0.06715212
Fumble Recoveries	0.02569808
Fumble Return Yards	-0.02105541
Fumble Return TDs	-0.03103474
Interception Return TDs	-0.05207392
Interception Return Yards	-0.05874961
Interceptions	-0.06762312
40 Yard Dash	-0.09182767
3 Cone Drill	-0.10974221
Pass Deflections	-0.12298169
Shuttle Drill	-0.12732362
Assisted Tackles	-0.21016598
Sacks	-0.21338467
Forced Fumbles	-0.2196645
Games Played	-0.22834525
Tackles for Loss	-0.24821472
Total Tackles	-0.27629769
Solo Tackles	-0.28092945

PC1 includes all of these statistics and measurements, but at varying degrees of importance. Whether or not the correlation is negative or positive is irrelevant at the moment; we are only concerned with the strength of the correlation. Variables shaded in grey have a ±0.20 or greater correlation to PC1 and are basically the only relevant measurements. Among the insignificant variables (not shaded) are randomly occurring big plays (e.g. fumble recoveries and return TDs), and non-normalized NFL

Combine measurements. Notice that all the weight-normalized Combine measurements (except for bench press) are relatively strongly correlated. Likewise tackles, sacks, and game experience are the most strongly correlated NCAA stats. Logically, this makes sense. Based on this analysis, athleticism seems to only matter within the context of the size of the athlete. Additionally, "*fluke*" plays in college (i.e. recoveries, return yards, and return TDs) don't appear to matter as much for a defensive end. So in summary, PC1 seems to be composed of measurements and stats that also logically seem important for predicting a defensive end's success in the NFL. But, does it actually predict anything? To test PC1 as a predictor of NFL pass rushing success, I plotted PC1 versus NFL career sacks per game, for each of the 82 defensive ends (Figure 4).

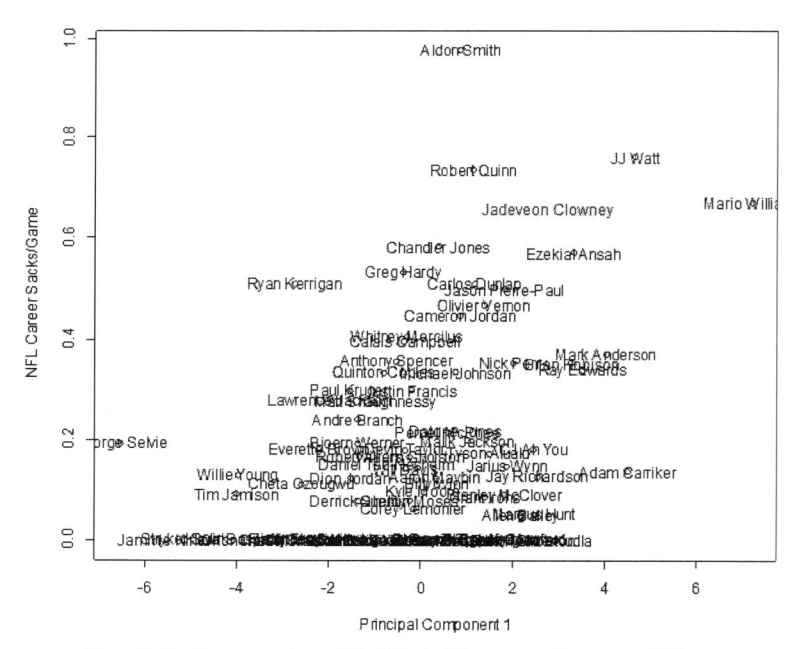

Figure 4: Our first composite variable (Principal Component 1) vs career NFL sacks per game. The upper limits for NFL sacks per game increases with increasing PC1.

Notice how as PC1 increases, so does the upper *limit* of career NFL sacks per game. Some names that appear along the upper limits include: Ryan Kerrigan, Greg Hardy, Chandler Jones, JJ Watt, Aldon Smith, and Mario Williams. It appears that these players realized their *potential* predicted from PC1, while players like Adam Carriker did not.

So let's think about the 2014 NFL draft, and one of the most discussed prospects in that class: Jadeveon Clowney. In Figure 4, you can see Jadeveon Clowney's name highlighted in red. His PC1 scoring landed him somewhere between Ziggy Ansah and Robert Quinn… quite impressive company. But, move directly down the figure to some of the lower responding percentiles, and you will see names like Jarius Wynn and Stanley McClover. This again highlights the objective of this chapter. I feel that PCA did a pretty decent job of objectifying a prospect's max potential, and PCA helps in identifying, quantitatively, what metrics are most important with a multivariate predictive model. But, PCA still does not help with the multitude of other unmeasured variables and unidentified factors that can limit a prospect's potential as a pro.

Although PC1 is far from being able to predict anything confidently, the purpose of this analysis is to better understand the potential of a prospect. When drafting a player with a high draft pick, a GM and the organization is betting on potential. In my opinion, it is imperative to objectively quantify the potential value and risk associated with that pick. When deciding on a first round pick, you'll be faced with many questions. Is Mario Williams a once-in-a-generation prospect? I believe he is. Will Adam Carriker be a household name, or is he just a big strong productive guy with a motor? I think his career statistics answer that question. The utility of using PCA and other ordination techniques is that it can help us make sense of data sets that before seemed extremely, confusing, variable, and *noisy*. Gambling the franchise on a player's potential is part of what makes the NFL draft so exciting. However, I think by using quantitative tools from other scientific disciplines, GMs could lower the stakes a bit. ☺

Quantifying the potential of Jadeveon Clowney using Quantile Regression

Extraordinary amounts of data go into evaluation an NFL prospect. The NFL combine, pro days, college statistics, game tape breakdown, and even personality tests can all play a role in predicting a player's future in the NFL. Once the top rated high school talent in the country, Jadeveon Clowney retained that distinction through 3 years in college football's most dominant conference, and is now an All-Pro with the Houston Texans. But, heading into the 2014 NFL Draft, there was much debate over Clowney's potential in the NFL. All prospects have a proverbial *"ceiling"* and a *"floor"*, which represent the maximum and lowest potential that a prospect could realize, respectively. And the most important question for the Texan's GM was: "Is his talent worth gambling millions of dollars, and the 1st overall pick on?" Using the same dataset from the previous chapter, I'll use Quantile Regression to clarify what Jadeveon Clowney's potential may be in the NFL.

> Note: I explain the Quantile Regression in more depth in previous chapters, including *The physiology behind the NFL Combine*.

Much more goes into assessing a player's pro potential than the combine, and the previous chapter illustrated just how many variables can. Using the PCA from the aforementioned chapter, I built a model to predict NFL production for defensive ends using the variables deemed statistically "most important" by the PCA. I then performed a Quantile Regression to explore what the "*ceiling*" and "*floor*" may be for defensive end prospects in the NFL. Of all metrics included in the PCA, the following appear to be the only significant measures in PC1 (Table 1):

Combine Results (weight normalized)	**NCAA Statistics**
Broad jump	Solo tackles
Vertical leap	Total tackles
40 yard dash	Tackles for loss
Shuttle	Games played
3 cone drill	Forced fumbles
Weight	Sacks
	Assisted tackles

Table 1: Significant variables chosen through PCA. All except for Games played and Assisted tackles were included in a multiple regression.

In the previous chapter on PCA, using Principal Component 1(PC1) as a predictor of NFL sacks per game did not prove very effective. However, using PC1 to inform me of what measures should be included into a predictive metric, could be. To build a predictive model, I performed a multiple regression using all the significant measures listed in Table 1, except for games played and assisted tackles.

> Note: To account for games played, I normalized solo tackles, total tackles, tackles for loss, forced

fumbles, and sacks per NCAA game played. Additionally, I did not include assisted tackles because I felt that using both solo and total tackles already did so.

I performed the multiple regression using these 11 measures as predictor variables for: Career NFL sacks + tackles for loss per game. Admittedly, there are better ways to quantify a defensive end's value in the NFL. The multiple regression returned the following correlation: $R = 0.704$ and $R^2 = 0.496$.

I used the following regression equation from the statistical output to predict "Career NFL sacks + tackles for loss per game" for each of our 82 defensive ends (the same dataset used in the previous chapter):

"Career NFL sacks + tackles for loss per game" =

-3.294 + (0.0640 * 40) + (0.00664 * **Vertical Leap**) - (0.000392 * **Broad Jump**) - (0.255 * **Shuttle**) + (0.439 * **3-Cone Drill**) + (0.551 * **NCAA tackles for loss per game**) - (0.579 * **NCAA sacks per game**) + (0.320 * **NCAA solo tackles per game**) - (0.138 * **NCAA total tackles per game**) - (0.00327 * **Body Weight**) + (0.00181 * **NCAA forced fumbles per game**)

I used this equation to calculate a predicted "sacks + tackles for loss per game" for each prospect. I then plotted the predicted number vs. the actual NFL "sacks + tackles for loss per game" that each player recorded in their careers (Figure 3).

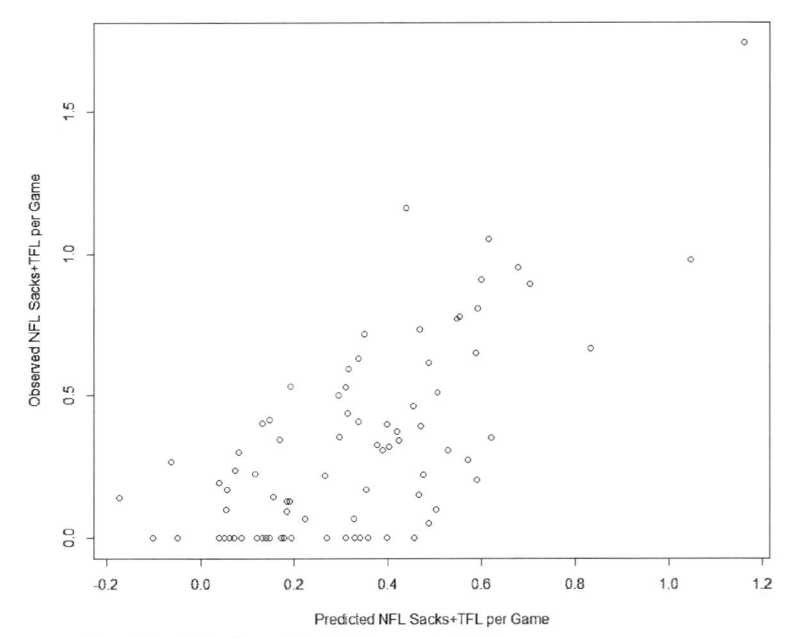

Figure 1: Predicted vs Observed Sacks+TFL per game in the NFL.

Looking at Figure 1, we can see that there is a general correlative trend, but nothing definitive or compelling. However, when I perform a Quantile Regression using the 25th, 50th, 75th, and 95th percentiles, the *picture* becomes a bit clearer (Figure 2).

The 50th percentile, or 0.5 quantile, is what linear regressions traditionally set to establish the correlation between the predictor and the mean response. However, an NFL GM may be more interested in the potential *"ceiling"* (95th or 75th) or *"floor"* (25th or lower) of a prospect that they are gambling millions on. In Figure 2, we can visualize this by observing the linear correlations at each quantile. Players like Whitney Mercilus, "Ziggy" Ansah, Robert Quinn, and JJ Watt fell along the 95th quantile of observed NFL production, meaning that they undoubtedly realized their potential as predicted by this model. Mario Williams, Brian Robison, and Anthony Spencer fell along the median quantile, or 50th percentile, meaning that they neither exceeded nor disappointed, statistically speaking. Jadeveon Clowney's name is highlighted in red in Figure 4. Clowney's career Sacks + TFL per game in the NFL (as of Summer 2017) is 1.26, landing him approximately in the 95th percentile, along with Watt and Ansah. Clowney has clearly exceeded his predicted value of approximately 0.74.

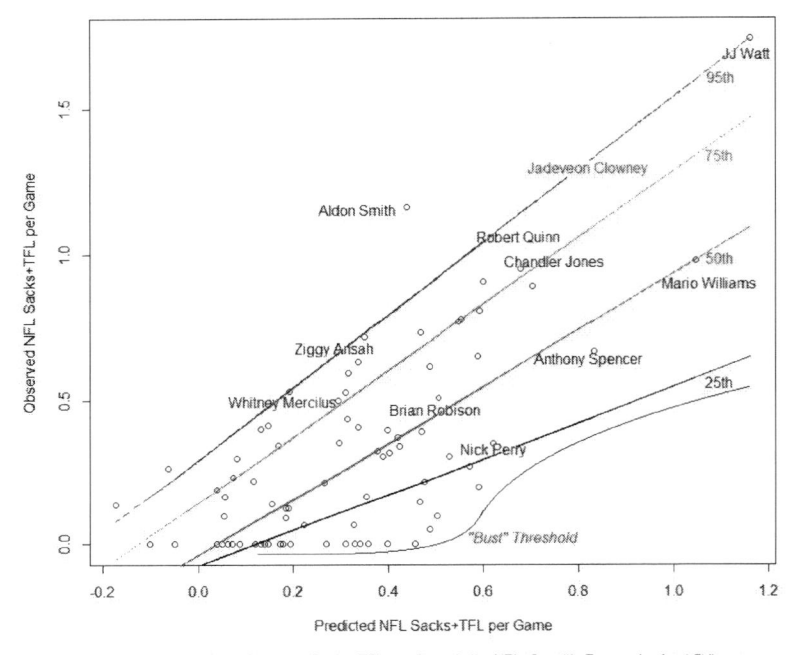

Figure 2: Predicted vs Observed Sacks+TFL per Game in the NFL. Quantile Regression best-fit lines are overlaid for the 95, 75, 50, and 25th percentiles.

Despite the success of players like Watt and Clowney, there remains a tremendous amount of "busts" in this dataset. Specifically, there are many "busts" in players predicted to record below a threshold of approximately 0.6 sacks+TFL per NFL game. This is an interesting and potentially helpful utility of using Quantile Regression in talent evaluations. Quantile Regression does not *only* look at the average response, but also can highlight the attributes of those players who exceed what is predicted, and those who fail to.

Quantile Regression helps to address the large amount of variability within these Combine datasets. It is not currently possible to measure attributes like motivation, dedication, work ethic, or focus. However, with techniques like PCA and Quantile Regression, we may be able to better identify those variables that we simply cannot attach a measurement to.

Quantifying Jadeveon Clowney's Combine Using Probabilistic Distributions

Heading into the 2014 NFL Draft, much of the debate over Clowney focused on his work ethic, dedication, and professionalism. However, I don't recall Clowney's athleticism ever being called into question. In fact, the consensus opinion was that Clowney was a *generational talent*, with character concerns. While I had seen his highlight videos, and I knew he was on his high school sprint team, I was still intrigued by the question of "Is Clowney's athleticism actually that rare?" But, how could I analyze that?

This chapter will serve as another case study aiming to objectively determine exactly how rare Jadeveon Clowney's athleticism is using Probabilistic Distributions. Probability Ranking allows me to identify the *probability* of finding a given athlete's level of athleticism. For instance, I probability ranked 40 yard dash times for 341 defensive ends from 1999-2014 (The table below shows the top 50). In this example, Jadeveon Clowney's 40 yard dash time of 4.53 seconds exhibited a probability rank of 99.12, meaning that Clowney's speed is in the 99.12th percentile of all DEs over this time span.

Note: I used the equation $P = 100 \times i /(n + 1)$ to rank combine drill performance, where i is the rank number of the data point, n is the total number of data points in the set, and P is the probability rank of that value, i.

Year	Name	College	Height (in)	Weight (lbs)	40 Yard Dash (secs)	Probability Rank
2002	Bryan Thomas	Alabama-Birmingham	77	266	4.47	99.71
2002	Dwight Freeney	Syracuse	73	266	4.48	99.41
2014	Jadeveon Clowney	South Carolina	77	266	4.53	99.12
2009	Lawrence Sidbury	Richmond	75	266	4.53	99.12
2013	Cornelius Washington	Georgia	76	265	4.55	98.53
2012	Nick Perry	Southern California	75	271	4.55	98.53
2002	Derrius Monroe	Virginia Tech	76	269	4.56	97.95
2000	Adalius Thomas	Southern Mississippi	75	270	4.56	97.95
2004	Isaac Hilton	Hampton	76	267	4.57	97.36
2014	Larry Webster	Bloomsburg	78	252	4.58	97.07
2005	David McMillan	Kansas	75	262	4.58	97.07
2005	Brady Poppinga	BYU	75	259	4.59	96.48
2013	Dion Jordan	Oregon	78	248	4.6	96.19
2013	Corey Lemonier	Auburn	75	255	4.6	96.19
2006	Kamerion Wimbley	Florida State	76	248	4.61	95.60
2013	Margus Hunt	Southern Methodist	80	277	4.62	95.31
2011	Robert Quinn	North Carolina	76	265	4.62	95.31
2006	Mark Anderson	Alabama	76	254	4.62	95.31
2006	Ryan LaCasse	Syracuse	75	257	4.62	95.31
2004	Jason Babin	Western Michigan	75	260	4.62	95.31
2004	Bobby McCray	Florida	78	255	4.62	95.31
2014	Jackson Jeffcoat	Texas	75	247	4.63	93.55
2013	Ezekial Ansah	Brigham Young	77	271	4.63	93.55
2011	Ugo Chinasa	Oklahoma State	77	264	4.63	93.55
2009	Brian Orakpo	Texas	75	263	4.63	93.55
2009	Stryker Sulak	Missouri	77	251	4.63	93.55
2006	James Wyche	Syracuse	78	262	4.63	93.55
2003	Shurron Pierson	South Florida	74	243	4.63	93.55
2007	Gaines Adams	Clemson	77	258	4.64	91.50
2010	Everson Griffen	Southern California	76	273	4.65	91.20
2009	Everette Brown	Florida State	74	256	4.65	91.20
2008	Vernon Gholston	Ohio State	75	266	4.65	91.20
2007	Jacob Ford	Central Arkansas	76	249	4.65	91.20
2004	Nathaniel Adibi	Virginia Tech	75	254	4.65	91.20
2004	Reggie Torbor	Auburn	74	254	4.65	91.20
2002	Will Overstreet	Tennessee	75	259	4.65	91.20
2005	Andre Frazier	Cincinnati	77	234	4.66	89.15
2012	Andre Branch	Clemson	76	259	4.67	88.86
2011	Patrick Kerrigan	Purdue	76	267	4.67	88.86
2007	Brian Robison	Texas	75	259	4.67	88.86
2003	Jerome McDougle	Miami	74	264	4.67	88.86
2002	Carlos Hall	Arkansas	76	259	4.67	88.86
1999	Melvin Bradley	Arkansas	73	269	4.67	88.86
2014	Marcus Smith	Louisville	75	251	4.68	87.10
2012	Whitney Mercilus	Illinois	76	261	4.68	87.10
2011	Jabaal Sheard	Pittsburgh	75	264	4.68	87.10
2010	Carlos Dunlap	Florida	78	278	4.68	87.10
2012	Quinton Coples	North Carolina	78	284	4.69	85.92
2009	Michael Johnson	Georgia Tech	79	266	4.69	85.92
2007	Baraka Atkins	Miami	77	271	4.69	85.92

To explore how Jadeveon Clowney's athleticism compared historically to other defensive ends, I probability ranked the most impressive individual drills and overall workouts of 82 defensive ends from 1999-2014 (this is the same dataset that was used in the previous two chapters). I applied a Weibull ranking to the following Combine measurements for all 82 players: 40 yard dash time, bench press, vertical leap, broad jump, short shuttle run, and 3-cone drill. This probability ranking revealed that Clowney's 40 yard dash time was very fast historically, while his overall combine performance was impressive, but fairly consistent with the decade's top performers. In Table 1 below, I list the NFL Combine measurements for six high draft picks at defensive end. Table 2 lists these same six defensive ends, along with their associated probability ranks among the entire class of 82 defensive ends:

Combine Results

	Ezekial Ansah	JJ Watt	Robert Quinn	Aldon Smith	Jason Pierre-Paul	Mario Williams	Jadeveon Clowney
Height (in)	77	77	76	76	77	79	77
Weight (lbs)	271	290	265	263	270	295	266
40 Yard	4.63	4.81	4.62	4.74	4.71	4.7	4.53
Bench Press	21	34	22	20	19	35	21
Vert Leap (in)	34.5	37	34	34	30.5	40.5	37.5
Broad Jump (in)	118	120	116	118	115	120	124
Shuttle	4.26	4.21	4.4	4.5	4.67	4.37	4.25
3Cone	7.11	6.88	7.13	7.19	7.18	7.21	7.27

Table 1: Raw combine results for 7 high profile DEs.

Probability Rank of Combine Results out of 82 Defensive Ends

	Ezekial Ansah	JJ Watt	Robert Quinn	Aldon Smith	Jason Pierre-Paul	Mario Williams	Jadeveon Clowney
Height (in)	59	59	35	35	59	94	59
Weight (lbs)	63	93	43	36	61	96	46
40 Yard	90	51	94	63	70	76	99
Bench Press	20	90	29	16	11	93	20
Vert Leap (in)	64	83	59	59	16	96	87
Broad Jump (in)	67	78	54	67	48	78	90
Shuttle	87	95	63	40	7	73	90
3Cone	75	99	72	60	63	54	39
Average Rank	**66**	**81**	**56**	**47**	**42**	**83**	**66**

Table 2: Probability ranking out of entire class of 82 for each combine drill and cumulative combine workout.

Jadeveon Clowney's 40 yard dash time of 4.53 registered in the 99th percentile of all defensive ends. Likewise, Clowney's leaping ability (vertical and broad), and his shuttle run time were in the 90th percentile of the class. However, Clowney's height, weight, bench press, and 3-cone drill were ranked average-below average within the class. This lowered Clowney's cumulative *Average Rank* for all Combine metrics to 66. For a comparison, Mario Williams had the highest cumulative *Average Rank* at 83. Ziggy Ansah actually shared an *Average Rank* of 66 with Clowney. The chart below displays where Clowney's *Average Rank* places him within the entire class of defensive ends (Figure 1):

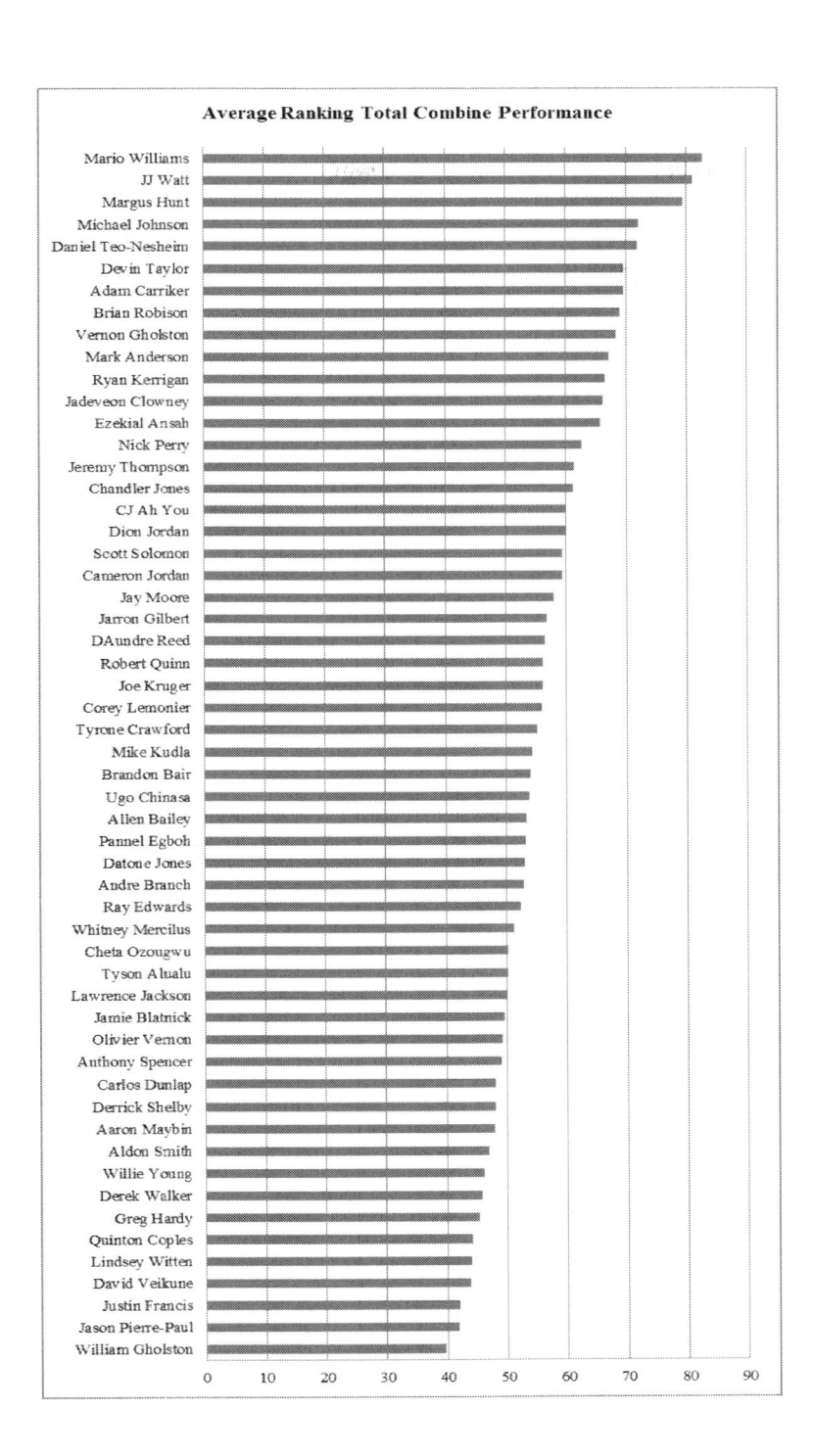

Average Ranking Total Combine Performance

Mario Williams	~82
JJ Watt	~80
Margus Hunt	~78
Michael Johnson	~72
Daniel Teo-Nesheim	~71
Devin Taylor	~69
Adam Carriker	~69
Brian Robison	~68
Vernon Gholston	~67
Mark Anderson	~66
Ryan Kerrigan	~66
Jadeveon Clowney	~65
Ezekial Ansah	~64
Nick Perry	~62
Jeremy Thompson	~61
Chandler Jones	~60
CJ Ah You	~60
Dion Jordan	~59
Scott Solomon	~59
Cameron Jordan	~58
Jay Moore	~57
Jarron Gilbert	~57
DAundre Reed	~56
Robert Quinn	~55
Joe Kruger	~55
Corey Lemonier	~55
Tyrone Crawford	~54
Mike Kudla	~54
Brandon Bair	~53
Ugo Chinasa	~53
Allen Bailey	~53
Pannel Egboh	~52
Datone Jones	~52
Andre Branch	~52
Ray Edwards	~52
Whitney Mercilus	~51
Cheta Ozougwu	~50
Tyson Alualu	~50
Lawrence Jackson	~50
Jamie Blatnick	~49
Olivier Vernon	~49
Anthony Spencer	~49
Carlos Dunlap	~48
Derrick Shelby	~48
Aaron Maybin	~47
Aldon Smith	~46
Willie Young	~45
Derek Walker	~45
Greg Hardy	~45
Quinton Coples	~44
Lindsey Witten	~44
David Veikune	~43
Justin Francis	~42
Jason Pierre-Paul	~41
William Gholston	~40

Figure 1: Average Probability Rank for cumulative combine performance

This is actually pretty impressive company. Among the players ranked ahead of Clowney, are JJ Watt, a future Hall of Famer, and Margus Hunt, a former world class track-and-field athlete. Of the players ranked below Clowney, Chandler Jones is a member of possibly the most athletic family in sports (see Jon and Arthur Jones), and Robert Quinn a former NFC sack leader. So while Jadeveon Clowney may not be a "*generational talent*", he is undeniably an elite athletic specimen who has produced in the NFL at an All-Pro level.

In Conclusion

If all NFL prospects eventually reach the athletic limits of human potential, will the NFL Combine even matter? It seems that, theoretically, as speed, strength, explosiveness, and agility improves across all players in the NFL, team success will depend upon less intangible attributes like scheme, intelligence, spatial awareness, coordination, and creativity. However, while there exists an athletic spectrum among players, there is extreme success in taking advantage of athletic advantages. Ever wonder why Sean Payton and Bill Belichick seem to "*get the most out of players?*" One of the reasons is that they both realize the importance in exploiting athletic mismatches. This entire book has focused on the most controlled metrics of athleticism. But moving forward, there will be great opportunities in identifying and capitalizing on specific athletic matchups, on a play-by-play basis. And hopefully, this book will motivate some of the future sports minds.

This book is dedicated to my family and friends for always supporting me. And para el amor de mi vida, Jannie.

Made in the USA
Middletown, DE
29 September 2018